E303 English Grammar in Context
Education and Language Studies
Level 3

The Open University

Book 2

Getting Inside English

Interpreting texts

Edited by K. A. O'Halloran

Units 8–11

Series editor: Caroline Coffin

This publication forms part of an Open University course E303 *English Grammar in Context*. Details of this and other Open University courses can be obtained from the Student Registration and Enquiry Service, The Open University, PO Box 197, Milton Keynes MK7 6BJ, United Kingdom: tel. +44 (0)870 333 4340, email general-enquiries@open.ac.uk

Alternatively, you may visit the Open University website at http://www.open.ac.uk where you can learn more about the wide range of courses and packs offered at all levels by The Open University.

To purchase a selection of Open University course materials visit http://www.ouw.co.uk, or contact Open University Worldwide, Michael Young Building, Walton Hall, Milton Keynes MK7 6AA, United Kingdom for a brochure. tel. +44 (0)1908 858785; fax +44 (0)1908 858787; email ouwenq@open.ac.uk

The Open University
Walton Hall, Milton Keynes
MK7 6AA

First published 2005. Second edition 2006.

Edited and designed by The Open University.

Typeset by The Open University.

Printed and bound in the United Kingdom by Halstan Printing Group, Amersham.

ISBN 978 0 7492 1776 1

2.1

Contents

Introduction to Book 2

It is common when travelling abroad to meet people who speak different languages. And it is natural for us to be interested in their languages and cultures, and how they differ from ours. People from other countries are often willing to talk about how they see English in relation to their native language – often via their experience of learning English. They may say things like:

> English is fairly easy to learn but only when you're starting off.

> I find English flexible.

In the first case, some might point out that English does not have many **inflections** – endings on nouns and verbs. So, for

> I love, you love, he/she loves, we love, they love

we only add an ending to the *he/she* form – *loves*. Russian and German, on the other hand, are heavily inflected, which means more inflections to remember. Learners often find English flexible since the same word form can be associated with different parts of speech. So verbs can function as nouns (*Let's have a* <u>drink</u>), adverbs can be verbs (*We've got to* <u>down</u> *our drinks*), and so on. In situations where languages are compared, people are happy to talk about the form of English and thus to talk about 'English', vast as it is, in general terms.

Yet in everyday life we never think about our own language in this way. We are too busy *using* language to communicate in particular situations, to make particular meanings, e.g. leaving a note for family members or our housemate to clear up, making an appointment on the phone to see the doctor, writing a report for the boss, reading the newspaper, getting home to continue writing the essay for the part-time course we are taking or reading a short story before we go to bed. Though we use English in very particular situations every day, situations which are actually very repetitive, it is much harder to talk about and compare how we make meaning in particular situations in our respective languages.

Book 1 provided insights into the differences between spoken and written English. Book 2 will help you understand how English varies according to the purposes of everyday situations. In particular, it will enable you to articulate how meaning is created in these situations. Take the following four fragments, for example. What types of usage do they show?

(a) Pod made a strange face, his eyes swivelled round towards Arriety. Homily stared at him, her mouth open, and then she turned. 'Come along, Arriety,' she said briskly, 'you pop off to bed, now, like a good girl, and I'll bring you some supper.'

(b) Since the mechanisms responsible for such correlations were not obvious, a more detailed empirical approach was used to investigate the effects of various weather factors on grasshoppers.

(c) Yeah and the girls that serve in there, there's three girls that serve in there, one works in the kitchen actually helping with the food, but the other two serve at the tables, they've all got qualifications but they can't get jobs.

(d) FOUR people were wounded in a gunfight between political extremists and police about 100 yards from Tony Blair in Cape Town yesterday after officers spotted men handing out guns to demonstrators baying for the Prime Minister's blood.

You probably had little trouble in deciding that these fragments of English come from different situations: *fiction, academic prose, conversation* and *news*, respectively. These fragments should tell you that, in our use and understanding of it, English is never a vast, uniform thing for us. English texts – spoken and written – are always related to particular situations of use and it is these four situations of use that we will be dealing with in this book in an effort to 'get inside' English. To understand why they differ we will be enriching the functional grammatical approach you were introduced to in Book 1. But to understand *how* they differ it is helpful to get a more bird's-eye perspective. You were able to recognise which situations of English the above fragments belonged to. But could you say accurately what the typical grammatical features are in fiction, conversation, academic writing and news? You may have some intuitions but you cannot know for sure without inspecting large databases of English from these situations.

We will therefore look again at corpus evidence to give us this bird's-eye view, and to do this we will draw upon the corpus evidence from your reference grammar for fiction, academic prose, conversation and news. Corpus-based grammars like your reference grammar enable us to avoid talking in the abstract about English as though it were a uniform thing; instead, they allow us to talk more accurately about English and how it is used in different social situations or contexts of use. To be able to do this is a major advance in linguistic study, an advance which has been facilitated by developments in computational databases and the ability to search quickly though them. Your student grammar refers to these four domains as registers. We shall refer to them in this course as the **Longman registers**. We will also make some use in this book of the 'parent grammar' to your student grammar, i.e. the *Longman Grammar of Spoken and Written English* (Biber et al., 1999). We shall reserve the term 'register' for the narrower definition found in systemic functional grammar. You will be introduced to this narrower version of the term in Unit 8.

There are four units in Book 2. In Unit 8, we will extend the functional framework to which you were introduced in Book 1 so you will be able to see why academic, news and conversational texts differ linguistically from one another in relation to different aspects of their social context. In Unit 9, we will examine the packaging and staging of information in news, fiction, academic prose and conversation. Unit 10 explores how text 'positions' readers by attempting to persuade them to adopt a particular point of view. In Unit 11, the focus turns to how meanings are constructed in line with a journalist's or novelist's 'angle of telling'.

In examining texts from the four Longman registers, you will enhance your skills of grammatical *description*. In locating texts in their situations of use and highlighting how English is used as a resource for meaning-making in fiction, news, conversation and academic writing, you will enhance your skills of *interpretation*. Overall, in becoming adept at describing and interpreting texts from academic prose, fiction, conversation and news, you will empower yourself as a communicator in English.

We started this introduction by giving you a travel scenario where people are interested in comparing the formal aspects of English with formal aspects of their own languages. There is nothing wrong with comparing languages formally – it is a very interesting thing to do – but you will see from this introduction (and you will already know from Book 1) that this course is much more about how English *functions*. We want you to be able to discuss how the forms of English are used to make meaning in particular situations. So while there is some focus on fiction and conversation, in Book 2 there is a significant focus on academic writing – an obvious benefit, since English is the primary medium of instruction on your university courses.

Another significant focus of Book 2 is news. Looking at news will illuminate a use of English which has enormous cultural significance, given that world events are conveyed in English news reporting much more than in any other language. Given this significance, an understanding of how English grammar and lexis are drawn on in order to turn material events into print news is a useful and interesting skill to possess. The more you know about how English is used to do this, the more articulate you can be in responding critically to the way events are reported. And if English is not your native language, by the end of Book 2 you will be in a better position to compare how events are turned into news in the English-speaking world with how this is done in your native language.

Unit 8

Ways of speaking – exploring linguistic variability

Prepared for the course team by Peter White

CONTENTS

Materials required

While studying this unit, you will need:

> the course reader
>
> the Activities CD-ROM
>
> the Concordancer and Corpus CD-ROM and *Corpus Tasks*.

Knowledge assumed

You should be familiar with the following before starting on this unit:

> shared situation
>
> spontaneity.

Introduction

Language is an endlessly variable phenomenon and we, as speakers, are linguistic chameleons. We change the way we talk – our use of types of words, phrases and structures – repeatedly throughout our daily lives, sometimes with only a moment's notice. We make these linguistic adjustments as we shift from casual conversation with friends or family to the greater formality required of, for example, a seminar presentation, a business meeting or asking a stranger for directions. Even within the family, we typically make significant adjustments as we converse with children or grandparents. And within the written mode there are lots of different 'grammars' – the 'grammar' of the email or letter to a close friend, the 'grammar' of a job application, the 'grammar' of an academic essay.

In Book 1 you explored this phenomenon of grammatical variability as it operates on the broadest scale – the grammatical shift which distinguishes the grammar of speech from that of writing. Now we will explore this variation in more detail, as observed in comparisons of conversation, fiction, journalism and academic prose.

Virtually all fluent speakers of a language are aware, in general terms, that such variation occurs in language, at least to the extent that they are aware that they must adjust the way they speak according to the social setting. But they will not necessarily be aware of just how substantial these changes can be. They certainly will not be aware of the precise nature of these adjustments. Our focus, then, in this and the following units will be upon these different styles or varieties of language – what are termed **registers** of language. Our purpose is to provide you with the means to identify both the obvious and the not-so-obvious aspects of these different styles and to understand why this variation occurs in the first place – that is, why certain grammatical features occur or are favoured in one register but do not occur or are not favoured in another.

Equipped with such a framework, you will be able to address many interesting linguistic issues, for example:

◆ What precisely is the 'academic style' (or register) of writing? How does it differ from other styles? Is it uniform or does it vary, for example, from discipline to discipline or according to whether the text is a student essay, a textbook or an expert journal article?

◆ What happens when expert topics (e.g. those relating to science, medicine or technology) are dealt with in popular, mass-market contexts such as newspaper reports or television features? What happens to the expert knowledge when it has to be communicated to a mass audience?

◆ How is it that certain types of writing seem 'conversational' or 'chatty' in style? That is, how is it possible to bring apparently spoken elements into a written text? What communicative ends are served by such a style? Why is it particularly favoured in advertising?

◆ Is there such a thing as a generalised fictional style? Do works of fiction display their own unique patterns of grammatical preferences? Do individual authors operate with their own linguistic 'fingerprints'?

◆ What happens when spoken language is pre-scripted – when, for example, radio and television newsreaders, political orators or television-drama actors speak words which were written down for them in advance? Will their language be more spoken or more written in style? Do supposedly naturalistic television dramas (e.g. soap operas) actually employ a natural, conversational style of language, or have some adjustments been made?

◆ Journalism is often held to involve a distinctive style of language. In English this is sometimes termed 'journalese'. Is this view valid? Is there, in fact, a journalistic register? If so, what grammatical features constitute it and what consequences might this style have for how information is communicated or how debates are conducted?

◆ Is the language employed to model conversational exchange in English as a foreign language textbooks 'natural'? Do the dialogues provided for students actually use the same grammar and vocabulary as occur in 'real' conversation? If not, why not? What might the negative consequence be of not employing 'real' language? What might the positive consequences be?

◆ Is there some connection between language and political success? Is it at least sometimes the case that those people who rise to positions of power or influence in the community have a particular way with words? Is their style of language such that it enables them to be particularly persuasive? Or, perhaps, is it the case that power corrupts linguistically – that the very powerful come to abuse language, to communicate in ways which oversimplify, discriminate or coerce?

Our topic in this unit, then, is the manner in which language varies according to its **context of use**. By context of use, we refer both to linguistically-relevant aspects of the social setting in which the language operates and to the communicative objectives served by the text – for example, it may function to argue a case, offer an explanation, give instructions, lay down the law, convey information, extract information from a witness, resolve a conflict, make friends, recount an amusing incident, and so on. We will demonstrate that this linkage between grammatical features and context of use is a systematic and frequently predictable one – that particular social factors and particular communicative objectives strongly favour the use of particular types of words and structures. Accordingly it is often possible for us, as students of the language, to work back from a text we have chosen to study to the context of use out of which it originated, to relate the occurrence of particular lexical and grammatical features in that text to specific features of the social situation in which it was originally produced.

As already indicated, in this unit we will broaden the scope of the discussion to go beyond the comparison between spoken and written language which was explored in Book 1. Specifically, we will compare and contrast examples of conversational, journalistic and academic language. Our purpose will be (a) to identify some of the distinctive or characteristic properties of these different registers of language, and (b) to relate these properties to the particular context of use in which these texts operate. We will begin by looking at three short text extracts which are set out below. Read them and try to identify any ways in which they are different from each other in the type of vocabulary used or the types of grammatical structures employed. Can you make any proposals as to how the grammatical style of each extract might in some way reflect features of its original context of use? More specific questions for you to consider are provided in Activity 1, which follows the texts.

Text 1

Dr [Jones], he's very good but as I say we don't run to a doctor for nothing, y'know what I mean. But we've had, had us jabs for flu. I got a lump on the back of my neck so we h... I had to have what was it called? [...] Antibiotics, and it must have helped it to burst or summat[1] and now of course it's pretty much gone. And that was it with me.

[¹ *summat*: colloquial or slang expression with a meaning similar to 'something', here indicating that the speaker is not entirely clear about what happened to the lump – *it burst or something like that*.]

Text 2

SALES of turnips are rocketing in China because the veg[1] is said to cure SARS[2].

They are used in herbal remedies sold to treat severe acute respiratory syndrome.

Wholesale prices of turnips in China's capital Beijing have shot up THIRTY PER CENT in a week amid fears over the deadly flu-like virus. Carrots, garlic and ginger are also included in the potions and shops have been selling out.

[[1] *veg* = short for 'vegetable'; [2] *SARS* = 'severe acute respiratory syndrome']

Text 3

The sex hormone estrogen is important for many physiologic processes. Prolonged stimulation of breast ductal epithelium by estrogen, however, can contribute to the development and progression of breast cancer, and treatments designed to block estrogen's effects are important options in the clinic. Tamoxifen and other similar drugs are effective in breast cancer prevention and treatment by inhibiting the proliferative effects of estrogen that are mediated through the estrogen receptor (ER).

ACTIVITY 1 (allow about 10 minutes)

(1) Can you reach conclusions about whether the texts were originally written or spoken?

(2) In what context/social setting do you think the texts were originally produced?

(3) What can you say about each extract's intended audience?

(4) Can you say anything about the relationship between the speaker/writer and those to whom the text was addressed? For example, were speaker/writer and addressee known to each other? Were they on friendly or familiar terms?

COMMENT

Perhaps the answers to at least some of these questions seem relatively obvious. Certainly there were some quite clear indicators that Text 1 was originally spoken while Text 3 was written. You may, for example, have identified the incomplete and the repeated words in Text 1 as indicators that it was a transcript of something originally spoken, and perhaps you thought the use of first- and second-person pronouns (*I, you*) and colloquial formulations such as *summat* in Text 1 also indicated this spoken mode.

You may also have felt that the presence of specialist terms such as *physiologic* and *ductal epithelium* in Text 3 indicated that it was designed for an expert audience, and that the absence of such terms in both Texts 1 and 2 similarly led to the conclusion that they were intended for a general readership or for non-experts.

You may have deduced that Text 2 was from a newspaper report. If you have a reasonable familiarity with English-language journalistic style, then perhaps this context was indicated to you by such 'journalistic' words and phrases as *rocketing*, *shot up*, *amid fears* and *deadly flu-like virus*. If you have an even closer knowledge of English-language journalistic style, the use of the shortened *veg* for 'vegetable' will have suggested that the text was from a tabloid newspaper rather than a broadsheet. ('Tabloid' newspapers, at least in Britain, are typically directed at a less well-educated audience and adopt a less formal, more familiar style than is found in 'broadsheets' such as *The Times* or *The Guardian*.)

In addition, you may have felt that you could make predictions about the relationship between those involved in these communicative events – that, for example, the relationship between the speaker and the addressee of Text 1 was one of familiarity or friendliness, while the impersonal language of Text 3 implied no such connection. Perhaps you also thought that the use in Text 1 of personal pronouns and the use of colloquial wordings and other casual modes of speech were indicative of this closer relationship.

All this indicates that even when we take such short extracts out of their original context we can still make quite reliable predictions about some aspects of their original context of use. We may only need a few sentences for such variation in words and grammatical structures to be revealed and hence for us, as analysts, to be able to identify a particular style or variety of language. This means that, in at least some areas, the relationship between a text's use of particular words and grammatical structures and that text's context of use will be relatively obvious and hence easy to identify.

OBJECTIVES OF THE UNIT

Part of what we will do in this and in following units will be to set out a systematic and comprehensive framework for identifying such 'obvious' indicators of a text's register, and for explaining just why they are so obvious. We will aim to explain why a particular linguistic element can be linked so directly to particular aspects of the text's situation of use.

We will also demonstrate, however, that some of these obvious indicators may not be quite so straightforward after all. Consider, for example, the indicators which we identified in Text 1. Certainly repeated words and false starts of the type we observed there point directly to the text having been originally spoken. But perhaps you also noticed the use of the first- and second-person pronouns, or the use of casual or colloquial wordings. Are these necessarily indicators of spokenness? Might we not find such elements in personal letters or emails between friends or close acquaintances? If so, this would suggest that they are not necessarily indicators of spokenness after all. Rather, they relate to the degree of social distance between the people communicating. In this regard, we would note that degrees of social distance may vary just as much between different types of written texts (for example, between a business letter and a personal email) as between a written and a spoken text (for example, between a business letter and a casual conversation between friends). Similarly, what do we make of the use of such casual wordings as the shortened *veg* in Text 2? Might we not expect such a colloquial style of language to occur in speech rather than in writing? And yet here it is in a written newspaper report. Does this suggest that written texts can contain 'spoken' elements – that it is possible to produce written texts which are 'conversational' in their vocabulary and/or grammar?

Beyond these more obvious aspects, we will also consider less obvious associations between vocabulary and grammar and the social situations in which that kind of language operates. We consider patterns in the use of words and grammatical structures – patterns that you will only be able to observe once you have grammatical knowledge of the type that this course seeks to develop. Specifically, we set out a framework to enable you to:

◆ understand and explain how particular categories of words, grammatical structures and text-organisation mechanisms function by reference to the social situation of their use

◆ identify different registers (styles) of language by reference to patterns of these words and structures

◆ reach conclusions about the distinctive communicative effects which are likely to follow from these patterns

◆ explain why these different registers vary in the way that they do, once again by reference to differences in their context of use.

In order to achieve this, we follow an approach developed within **systemic functional linguistics (SFL)**. The SFL approach enables us to go beyond simply proposing that social context and communicative objectives influence the style of language used (which is, after all, a relatively obvious point) to being able to specify much more precisely which aspects of the social context might influence or determine which aspects of the language are being used. Specifically, SFL proposes that the style of language used will reflect, or be influenced by (a) what is termed the **field** of the text (its subject matter), (b) what is termed its **tenor** (the social roles and relationships of those involved), and (c) what is termed its **mode** (the nature of the communication – for example, whether spoken or written). That is, under the framework we will be using here, it is possible to explain the use in a text of particular words or grammatical structures by reference to these three aspects. These notions are therefore key, and are set out here in more detail.

Field

Some aspects of the language found in a particular text or text type will be determined by the particular domain of experience which the text is depicting – its subject matter (for example, family life, religious observance, law enforcement, news reporting, medicine and public health, scientific research, philosophy, advertising, politics, car maintenance, content labelling on foodstuffs, cooking recipes, etc.). 'Field' can refer to both subject matter and situation of use: for example, if I utter the expression *cardiac arrest*, you will think of the medical register, the subject matter to which *cardiac arrest* belongs; but the following piece of speech – *Nurse ... scalpel ...* – also refers to the medical register, though more specifically the situation of use.

Tenor

Some aspects of the text will reflect (a) the persona, social role or personality of the speaker/writer, and (b) the relationship which holds between this speaker/writer and those with whom they are communicating.

Mode

Some aspects of the text will be determined by the nature of the text as a communicative event or action – for example, whether it took the form of writing or speech; whether it was spontaneously or non-spontaneously produced; whether it involved interaction between multiple speakers or was constructed by one writer or speaker in isolation; and so on.

Field, tenor and mode, then, are aspects of a text's context of use, and the type of field/tenor/mode determines the register: for example, a cooking recipe takes account of the situation of use (that we will be using the recipe in the kitchen, and so will alternate between the text and the stages of execution), the tenor (normally informal) and the mode (which is written, to capture the original chef's creation). They are aspects of the social world which directly influence which types of words, phrases and structures are used in texts. As these aspects vary (for example, as the subject matter varies from sport to economics, or the relationship between interlocutors varies from intimacy to social distance) then so too will the register vary.

SFL takes one step further with regard to register. It was noticed that each of these three situational aspects (field, tenor and mode) tends to be related to particular types of lexical and grammatical elements. For example, the field of the text will be reflected in the types of participants and processes which occur, while its tenor will be reflected in whether the text consists entirely of statements or, alternatively, also includes questions and/or commands. It is therefore possible to group lexical and grammatical elements according to whether they relate to, or reflect, the field, the tenor or the mode of the text. Specifically, those elements related to field (subject matter/domain of experience) are termed **experiential** meanings, those related to tenor (social roles and relationships) are termed **interpersonal** meanings, and those related to mode (nature of text as communicative event) are termed **textual** meanings. Because these different types of elements have these different functions, in the broadest sense of the term, they are termed **metafunctions**. Thus we have the following linkages:

In other books or courses, such as The Open University's second level English Language courses (U210 *The English Language: past, present and future* or U211 *Exploring the English Language*), you may have come across the term **ideational** to mean what is here referred to as experiential meaning.

Aspect of situation	Linguistic function (metafunction)
Field – subject matter/activity type	Experiential
Tenor – social roles and relationships of those involved in the communication	Interpersonal
Mode – nature of the text as a communicative process/its channel	Textual

With the framework in place, we should now be able to go back to our preliminary discussion of the three text extracts in Activity 1 and account more systematically for the styles of language we observed there. For example, in Text 1, vocabulary items such as *doctor, jabs for flu, lump, neck* and *antibiotics* are experiential elements which enable us to establish the text's field as being that of health care as experienced by an individual attending his/her local doctor. Similarly, its use of colloquial, casual and informal items (for example, *summat*) is an interpersonal feature of the text which enabled us to establish that the tenor was one in which the interlocutors were on familiar or friendly terms. Likewise, repetitions and false starts are textual features which enabled us to establish the mode as one in which the interlocutors are involved in spontaneous, face-to-face spoken conversation.

In the rest of this unit we will deal with tenor before going on to explore field and mode, in Sections 3 and 4 respectively.

❷ LINGUISTIC INDICATORS OF TENOR – THE INTERPERSONAL

In order to explore this analytical framework we will examine further examples of texts drawn from conversational interaction, from journalism and from academic research, including longer versions of the texts from which the three extracts above were drawn. We will begin by investigating some key interpersonal linguistic features – that is, those associated with tenor.

As has been shown, tenor relates to the roles and relationships of those involved in the communication. It is important to stress that, in talking about tenor, we are concerned with the social roles and relationships that are enacted in a particular text, rather than with any roles or relationships that might be seen as pre-existing. To illustrate this, consider the situation of a parent and child. We might think that such a situation involves a relatively fixed relationship, with the parent in the socially-dominant role and the child in the subordinate role. However, if we observed the actual verbal interactions between these two individuals over time, we might well observe considerable variation in the nature of the language used, for example, by the parent as he/she acted in a more or a less authoritative or authoritarian way. On some occasions the parent might adopt language which indicates that he/she effectively has absolute power over the child (for example, *Go to bed at once; there's no more television for you for the rest of the week*), while on other occasions the parent might use language indicating that his/her power is less absolute and that he/she is more on the same level as the child (for example, *What do you think about us doing some work in the garden? It's a really nice day to be out in the sunshine*). Accordingly, we would need to allow for the possibility that the precise nature of the relationship between the parent and the child can vary according to circumstances or over time, with the actual language likewise varying as it is used to construct a particular relationship at a given time and place.

What this means is that, strictly speaking, tenor relates not to some generalised notion of personalities, roles and relationships but to what is indicated about the personalities, roles and relationships of the people communicating by their use of language in a specific text.

In investigating how this interpersonal aspect of language reflects social roles and relationships, we will be interested in the following three broad issues:

◆ whether the language indicates that those involved are equal in terms of social status or power, or whether they are unequal

◆ whether the language indicates that those involved are on familiar, friendly or intimate terms, or whether it indicates that they are unknown to each other or are in some other way socially distant

◆ what the language indicates about the sort of social role being performed by the speaker(s)/writer(s) and what it indicates about their personality or identity.

2.1 Relative social status (equality/inequality) in spoken interaction

We first consider the issue of **relative social status** (equality/inequality) and how this is revealed through language. This phenomenon is best observed in interactive types of texts such as spoken dialogues where multiple participants can be seen adopting positions of greater or lesser social standing relative to each other. It can also be observed, but to a lesser extent, in non-interactive texts such as most forms of writing since here, with just one communicator, it is not possible to observe relative differences in power or authority between communicative participants. However, note that even in written monologues it is still possible for writers to present themselves as more or less authoritative or expert.

Relative social status is revealed by whether or not the people communicating have equal access to, or make equal use of, various key meanings and communicative functions, for example:

◆ whether they are equally able to make statements, ask questions or give directions

◆ whether they are able to make use of similar terms of address when referring to each other (for example formal titles such as 'Sir', 'Ma'am', 'Dr', 'Professor', 'Your Excellency', 'Mr', 'Mrs' as opposed to given names)

◆ whether they are equally able to determine the direction the conversation takes by, for example, choosing or changing the topic

◆ whether they are equally able to pass judgement or make assessments.

ACTIVITY **2** (allow about 10 minutes)

Read the following text (an extended version of Text 1 on p. 10) and think about the relative social status of each speaker. Then answer the questions that follow.

Key to transcription: ‖ ... ‖ indicates that the current speaker and the following speaker overlap here, i.e. both talk simultaneously; '+' indicates that the word has been cut short – the complete word has not been fully articulated or could not be transcribed owing to some overlap or interruption.

Text 4

SPEAKER 1 How do you find the local GP?

SPEAKER 2 Oh he's all right.

SPEAKER 1 Which ... which surgery are you at?

SPEAKER 2 Er [Name-of-Road] Street.

SPEAKER 1 [Name-of-Road] Street.

SPEAKER 2 Mm. Dr [Name-of-Doctor], he's very good but as I say we don't run to a doctor for nothing, y' know what I mean. But we've had <coughs> had us jabs for flu. I got a lump on the back of my neck so we h+ I had to have what was it called?

SPEAKER 3 Antibiotics

SPEAKER 2 Antibiotics and it must have helped it to burst or summat and now of course it's pretty much gone. And that was it with me.

[...]

SPEAKER 2 I had skin cancer. I'd been digging in the garden and and I don't know whether I scratched myself with a <pause> 'cos I was doing my <pause> I don't whether a s+ a thorn caught me on the nose and then I'd been digging

SPEAKER 1 Mm.

SPEAKER 2 Cats and all sorts had been digging about, I hate cats, and it wouldn't heal up and it was going on and I was getting cream cream on my nose - it never ha+ healed up you see. So I went to the doctor's and they looked at it down the infirmary. Then they had to have those all these specialists round you you know and I thought, Why the heck am I seeing other people. Anyway they had to have ten

SPEAKER 3 She had to have ten sessions of radiotherapy

SPEAKER 2 On my nose.

SPEAKER 1 Right. When was this? When was this?

SPEAKER 2 Last year wasn't it?

SPEAKER 3 No two.

SPEAKER 2 Was it?

SPEAKER 3 Two years.

SPEAKER 2 Two years ago.

SPEAKER 1 Two years ago.

SPEAKER 3 Two years

SPEAKER 1 How did you feel about that when you found out?

SPEAKER 2 Oh I thought well it'll be, you know

SPEAKER 3 Well she was definitely scared.

SPEAKER 1 Mm.

SPEAKER 3 Because they had to take a biopsy you know cut out and stitch it up again and then er it proved positive so she had to come and

SPEAKER 2 Ten ten weeks ten days wasn't it?

SPEAKER 3 Ten days yeah.

SPEAKER 2 Now the first one I was all right but the second one it made me feel a little bit sick 'cos you wasn't <pause> it was only a couple of minutes on this thing ‖ you know <overlap>

SPEAKER 3   ‖ It was radiation, effects of radiation, you just just put a lead mask over leaving the area

SPEAKER 2 Yeah.

SPEAKER 3 and then bombard with

SPEAKER 2 Yeah. Cos you've got to protect your eyes

SPEAKER 1 Mmm.

SPEAKER 2 and everything else. But they was very very good down there wasn't they at the infirmary.

SPEAKER 1 Mmm.

(Collins Cobuild Bank of English: subcorpus = brspok/UK)

Can you reach any conclusions about the types of roles being played by the speakers and the relationships between them based on any similarities or differences in their use of language? Can you identify linguistic inequalities which might point to inequalities in the social standing of the three speakers? Does one or other of the speakers seem to be more dominant or more in control of the conversation? Based on this analysis, can you place the interaction in a particular social setting? In what circumstances might you expect to encounter an exchange of this type? (You might like to write some answers in your notebook before reading the comments below.)

COMMENT

In conducting this type of analysis, one of the first aspects of language to investigate is the basic communicative functions being performed by the various speakers. Here we need to examine precisely what the speakers are doing with their language and how they position themselves and those they address interactively. For example, by using statements, speakers provide information, and thereby (a) position themselves as possessing material worthy of communication, and (b) position those they address as in some way needing or lacking this material. They thus adopt for themselves the role of informational providers and assign to those they address the role of informational receivers. Similarly, by using questions, speakers present themselves as seeking information from their addressee, or at least as seeking some response from them. They thus reverse the position which applies in the case of statements, adopting for themselves the role of informational receiver and placing the addressee in the role of provider. By using commands the speaker adopts a rather different type of communicative role, not dealing with informational content but rather seeking to control or influence the behaviour of those addressed. They thus adopt for themselves the role of demander or seeker of some action or service while placing the addressee in the role of provider of that action or service.

In the case of this text, there are some marked differences at the level of the communicative and interactive roles adopted by the speakers.

Speaker 1 is in the role of seeker of information as he/she largely confines him/herself to asking questions and offering feedback in support of the statements by Speakers 2 and 3. He/she makes no statements on his/her own behalf. He/she does not interrupt, or overlap with, the turns of the other two speakers once he/she has set in train a particular topic of conversation.

Speaker 2 is in the role of the primary provider of information. She spends most of the conversation making statements in reply to

Speaker 1's questions, although she does offer some questions on her own behalf (e.g. *I had to have what was it called?*). On one occasion she takes up the option of completing Speaker 3's turn:

SPEAKER 3 She had to have ten sessions of radiotherapy

SPEAKER 2 On my nose.

On one occasion she takes up the option of interrupting Speaker 3:

SPEAKER 3 Because they had to take a biopsy you know cut out and stitch it up again and then er it proved positive so she had to come and <interruption>

SPEAKER 2 Ten ten weeks ten days wasn't it?

Speaker 3 appears to make use of essentially the same linguistic options as Speaker 2. He/she makes statements and takes up options to interrupt the turn of Speaker 2. However, the dynamics of the conversation are such that his/her contributions largely take the form of responses to requests for informational assistance/clarification from Speaker 2 (rather than to questions from Speaker 1) and of contributions to clarify for Speaker 1 some aspect of Speaker 2's turns. These clarifications typically take the form of interruptions to Speaker 2. For example:

SPEAKER 2 ...Anyway they had to have ten <interruption>

SPEAKER 3 She had to have ten sessions of radiotherapy

[...]

SPEAKER 2 Oh I thought well it'll be, you know

SPEAKER 3 Well she was definitely scared.

This particular pattern of linguistic inequality is suggestive of a particular set of role relationships – namely that of interviewer and interviewee, with Speaker 1 in the interviewer role and Speaker 2 in the main interviewee role. The interviewer role is indicated by the fact that Speaker 1's contribution is confined to asking questions and offering supportive feedback. This exchange is different in important respects from casual conversational exchanges between equal communicative participants, such as friends or work colleagues, where there are no differences in terms of hierarchy in the workplace and where questions and statements will tend to be much more evenly distributed between participants. This exchange, in fact, occurred as part of an interview conducted for the purposes of linguistic research.

Certain conventionalised roles are indicated by these grammatical and interactional patterns. But what can we say of the power or relative standing of the interlocutors? Well, the situation with respect to power relations is somewhat complicated. Clearly the interviewer (Speaker 1) has the power to determine the direction of the exchange by means of his/her questions. And by these questions he/she clearly demonstrates the power to demand, or at least request, information from the other speakers. These powers are acquired by dint of the conventions of the interview as it operates today, as a standardised mode of interaction in many cultures. Yet, simultaneously, the interviewer surrenders the power to offer information. He/she forgoes the right to make any informational contribution to the exchange, handing this over to the interviewees.

The relationship between the two interview subjects (Speakers 2 and 3) seems to be essentially one of equality. They both make statements and each takes up the option to interrupt or overlap the other's turns.

2.2 Speaker/writer persona: power, expertise or authority

The above account demonstrates, in general terms, the methodology for analysing equality/inequality in multi-participant interactive texts – we observe the use of language by the various speakers in order to discover any consistent differences which can be seen relating to power, expertise or authority.

But what happens in the case of single-participant, non-interactive texts such as journalistic reports or academic articles? Here, as already shown above, the text is constructed by a single author (or possibly a group of authors) and so we no longer have the option of comparing and contrasting the different linguistic contributions of the various speakers. We therefore need to adjust our analytical methodology. We need to examine not how multiple participants interact with each other linguistically, but how individual authors present themselves to the reader. We need to consider whether, by their language, writers represent themselves as being authoritative, expert, powerful or otherwise holding a position of influence or high status in society. In essence we need to consider the **persona** being created in the text. This means looking at such issues as whether the writer employs language that can be seen as assertive or as demonstrating expertise, whether they present themselves as in a position to give advice to readers or to direct or control the actions of others, whether they present themselves as in a position to criticise or praise others, and so on.

ACTIVITY 3 (allow about 30 minutes)

Read the following two journalistic texts. As in the previous conversational text, they are also concerned with matters of human health. Then make notes in answer to the questions that follow. (Text 5A is a longer version of Text 2 on p. 11, discussed in Activity 1.)

Can you identify any systematic differences in the use of language in the two texts which might be seen as relating to the respective authors' expertise, authority or influence? What sort of journalistic persona is being performed by each of the authors? Does one of the authors seem to be operating with a higher social standing than the other? You might like to focus specifically on the issue of differences in communicative function which was explored above. That is, consider whether there are differences between the texts in terms of whether the authors provide factual information, pass judgements, ask questions, give advice, issue commands, or seek to direct the behaviour of others.

Text 5A

TURNIPS 'CURE SARS'

Demand for veg rockets in killer bug scare

SALES of turnips are rocketing in China because the veg is said to cure SARS.

They are used in herbal remedies sold to treat severe acute respiratory syndrome.

Wholesale prices of turnips in China's capital Beijing have shot up THIRTY PER CENT in a week amid fears over the deadly flu-like virus. Carrots, garlic and ginger are also included in the potions and shops have been selling out.

The global death toll from SARS rose to 153 yesterday. Nine were reported in Hong Kong – the most in one day there so far. They included a woman aged 34, who died while giving birth. The condition of the baby was not known.

China has been hit hardest by SARS, with 64 deaths.

One newspaper in the country has recommended dead silkworms in one remedy.

There is still no recognised cure for SARS, which has infected more than 3,300 people in at least 20 countries since it emerged in southern China last November.

However, a German company said yesterday it had developed a high-speed test for the virus.

Artus, based in Hamburg, said it could detect SARS in two hours.

Current checks can take up to ten days.

Artus said it would distribute the test free to laboratories worldwide.

Manager Thomas Laue said: 'It will be our share in controlling this plague.'

Seven people in Britain have been treated so far for SARS symptoms.

Four have recovered and been discharged from hospital.

It was revealed yesterday that one of the other three might have contracted the illness during a charity walk on the Great Wall of China.

Rob Blyde, 29, of Morningside, North Lanarkshire, became ill after returning to Scotland.

The newsagent and DJ went to China to raise funds for St Andrew's Hospice in Airdrie.

Last night he was in a stable condition at Wishaw General Hospital, Lanarkshire.

An eighth Briton is being treated for SARS in Indonesia.

The World Health Organisation has said SARS could be the first global epidemic of this century.

It has already killed 56 people in Hong Kong, 13 in Canada, 12 in Singapore, five in Vietnam, two in Thailand and one in Malaysia.

Many people in South East Asia wear surgical masks in a bid to avoid catching the bug.

(Adapted from Russell, *The Sun*, 16 April 2003)

Text 5B

For Hong Kong, a time for soul-searching

Hong Kong's Central Policy Unit has asked the University of Hong Kong for help in understanding why Hong Kong's international image has taken a beating since 1997. It is not the first time, nor will it be the last, that such worries have surfaced. In 1995, when Fortune magazine predicted the 'death of Hong Kong' after 1997, the reverberations echoed for years, and still echo. The battle with severe acute respiratory syndrome (Sars) has exposed all our latent weaknesses, ranging from the poverty of our leadership to the fragile bonds of trust with the mainland, which have been sorely strained by the central government's cover-up of the crisis.

How, then, to dig ourselves out of the deep hole in which we suddenly find our public and private sense of self-esteem? The CPU's attempt to track foreign media coverage is not such a bad idea. More often than not officialdom resorts to such studies in order to shift blame elsewhere, but accepting that Hong Kong does have an image problem is at least a first step towards finding solutions. Long before this study is completed, however,

Hong Kong will have to begin a process of soul searching that will rival the self-questioning that followed Hong Kong's return to China. However difficult, this exercise could also be immensely rewarding, because Hong Kongers will have to work at it both individually and collectively, from the humblest shop clerk to the grandest tycoons and high officials. We can, for example, start working in earnest to earn Hong Kong a reputation for quality of life by making it a clean city. Hygiene has suddenly become a huge issue in connection with Sars, and with one of the world's most densely packed cities. Hong Kong can no longer afford to be less than squeaky clean when it comes to public and private spaces. If the government cannot pay for all the cleanup needed, local business and neighbourhood groups should take up collections and pay extra to make sure that every surface gleams.

And let's not stop with simply washing up our homes, streets, and parks. After the man-made parts, come the air, land, and water, which have suffered as a result of Hong Kong's conurbation and its carelessness, as well as its inability to work out solutions with polluters on the mainland.

The integration issues run much deeper, of course. This crisis has exposed the danger created by the gulf in understanding and co-operation between Hong Kong and the Pearl River Delta. This must serve as a wake-up call that Hong Kong needs to get serious about the practical aspects of integration and ensure it becomes a day-to-day reality for ordinary people. The crisis has forced health officials to widen communication on infectious disease – efforts that could serve as an example for the wider community.

Out of crisis may come despair, but crisis can also lead to transformation.

(*South China Morning Post*, 15 April 2003)

COMMENT

Both texts can be seen as 'expert' to the extent that both authors present themselves as having some degree of knowledge in a topic area which is of broad interest to society in general. They both present themselves as providers of information to an audience which, presumably, is interested but lacks knowledge. It is, of course, a very generalised expertise, which would be possessed by virtually all mass-media news agencies.

It is probably obvious to you that, beyond this basic similarity, the two texts are examples of different types of journalism – the first is a factual news report and the second is an editorial. As a consequence, the two texts deal with rather different types of meanings. Text 5A presents a series of statements describing real happenings in the material world.

An editorial is an article expressing the opinion of the editors or publishers of the newspaper.

Text 5B does contain some factual information of this type, but its primary concern is with opinion – with passing negative judgements of the government and presenting an argument about how the people of Hong Kong should react to the crisis.

This difference in communicative functionality can be easily traced to differences at the linguistic level – specifically, differences in (a) the amount and type of evaluative language used, and (b) the use of meanings relating to obligation or necessity. Thus we observe that there are only two instances in the first text of evaluative language – when the disease is negatively characterised as a *killer bug* and as *deadly*. Even then, such evaluations can be classed as factual on the grounds that the disease's deadliness is an objectively observed property. In contrast, the second text contains lots of authorial opinions directed, most notably, at the Government of Hong Kong, at other institutions and at Hong Kong society generally. Thus, to cite just a few examples, Hong Kong's government is characterised as incompetent (*the poverty of our leadership*) and its recent handling of the SARS epidemic as dishonest (*the central government's cover-up of the crisis*). Hong Kong society in general is characterised as flawed or enfeebled (*our latent weaknesses*) and relations with mainland China as troubled (*the fragile bonds of trust with the mainland*). We can observe a similar marked contrast with respect to meanings relating to obligation/necessity. None occurs in Text 5A, while they occur repeatedly throughout Text 5B, for example:

Hong Kong will have to begin a process of soul searching

this exercise could also be immensely rewarding, because Hong Kongers will have to work at it both individually and collectively

Hong Kong can no longer afford to be less than squeaky clean

local business and neighbourhood groups should take up collections and pay extra to make sure that every surface gleams

This must serve as a wake-up call that Hong Kong needs to get serious about the practical aspects of integration

The two texts, then, are markedly different in these two aspects. But how do we interpret such differences in terms of the author's power, authority or status? Well, clearly – in assuming the right to instruct the people of Hong Kong in what they should do and think – the author of the second text presents him/herself as occupying a position of significant authority and status, and similarly in assuming the right to pass such strongly negative judgements of both Hong Kong society and the government. No such assumptions are made by the first text, which claims only the authority to provide a record of recent newsworthy events. The fact that these texts are articles in mass-circulation daily newspapers is also significant here. It would be one thing for us as private individuals to express such views to our friends or close acquaintances. But here the views contained in the second text are being very publicly communicated to the society as a whole. The authority being claimed by the second text is not simply that of holding and expressing such views but that of being entitled to do so in a very public and potentially influential manner. We should also note in this regard that these two textual modes (reporting versus commentating) are associated with clearly demarcated journalistic roles, at least for many journalistic organisations around the world, with these roles occupying different positions in the professional journalistic hierarchy. The function of recording events in the manner of the first text is conventionally associated with the general reporter role, a position with the lowest status in the professional hierarchy of journalism. In contrast, arguing, instructing and passing judgement in the manner of the second text is conventionally associated with the much-higher-status role of commentator, columnist or editorial writer.

This analysis shows how it is possible to reach conclusions about social standing in non-interactive texts. We discovered linguistic features in the texts which could plausibly be related to the text's persona – its level of authoritativeness and the social standing to which the author was laying claim. It should be noted that while we only focused on evaluative language and meanings of obligation/necessity, further types of meanings may also be relevant to such analyses. We looked at written texts, but the same methodology can be applied to non-interactive, single-party spoken texts such as political speeches, lectures, sermons and some types of television or radio advertisements. So the concept of persona can be applied to speakers as well as writers.

2.3 Social distance (degree of familiarity or connection)

We turn now to a second key aspect of the relationship between those involved in a communication – the degree of **social distance**, familiarity or connection between them. Here we are concerned with whether the language employed indicates that the communicative participants are more or less well known to each other (for example, as family members, friends or close acquaintances) or, alternatively, indicates they are not on familiar terms or are in some other way socially distant. Social closeness is indicated via what can be thought of as 'informal' language, for example:

◆ the use of colloquial, casual or slang vocabulary

◆ the use of more familiar terms of address such as given names, nicknames, pet names, etc.

◆ the use of reduced, abbreviated or elliptical forms of expression –
conflations such as *I'll, what'll, I'd've (I would have)*, etc., incomplete
clauses, etc.

ACTIVITY **4** (allow about 10 minutes)

In order to demonstrate how texts may vary in terms of social distance,
you are going to compare Texts 4 (pp. 18–19) and 5A (pp. 23–24) with
a further health-related text, this time an example of academic writing
(Text 6, below). Read all three, then consider the following questions.

In terms of social distance, what does the language suggest about the
relationships between the communicative participants? This means that
for Text 4 (the spoken interaction) you should consider the degree of
contact among the three speakers, while for Texts 5A (the news report)
and 6 below (the academic article) you should consider the degree of
contact between the author and his/her intended audience. Specifically,
try to identify any examples of informal language in the three texts.
(Please note that, for the purposes of this analysis, it is not necessary to
be familiar with the precise meanings of the specialist medical and
scientific terms that occur in the text.)

Text 6

The sex hormone estrogen is important for many physiologic
processes. Prolonged stimulation of breast ductal epithelium by
estrogen, however, can contribute to the development and
progression of breast cancer, and treatments designed to block
estrogen's effects are important options in the clinic. Tamoxifen and
other similar drugs are effective in breast cancer prevention and
treatment by inhibiting the proliferative effects of estrogen that are
mediated through the estrogen receptor (ER). However, these drugs
also have many estrogenic effects depending on the tissue and gene,
and they are more appropriately called selective estrogen receptor
modulators (SERMs). SERMs bind ER, alter receptor conformation,
and facilitate binding of coregulatory proteins that activate or
repress transcriptional activation of estrogen target genes.
Theoretically, SERMs could be synthesized that would exhibit nearly
complete agonist activity on the one hand or pure antiestrogenic
activity on the other. Depending on their functional activities,
SERMs could then be developed for a variety of clinical uses,
including prevention and treatment of osteoporosis, treatment and
prevention of estrogen-regulated malignancies, and even for
hormone replacement therapy. Tamoxifen is effective in patients
with ER-positive metastatic breast cancer and in the adjuvant
setting. The promising role for tamoxifen in ductal carcinoma-in-situ
or for breast cancer prevention is evolving, and its use can be

considered in certain patient groups. Other SERMs are in development, with the goal of reducing toxicity and/or improving efficacy.

> (Osborne et al., 2000, pp. 3172–86; quoted in PubMed website, 4 September 2003)

COMMENT

Text 4

Text 4 includes the following colloquial vocabulary and phrases:

> jabs, I got a lump (got rather than developed), summat, pretty much, Why the heck, a little bit sick (little bit does not occur as a term of measure in more formal language)

It also includes a relatively high number of contractions. For example:

> y'know, we've, I'd, don't, 'cos

This text also contains a number of grammatical structures which suggest either a regional dialect or a social-class dialect. For example:

> we've had us jabs for flu

> 'cos you wasn't

> they was very very good down there wasn't they at the infirmary

Such dialectal forms are also suggestive of informality and some degree of closeness.

Text 5A

There are just a couple of more clearly colloquial expressions in Text 2: veg as short for 'vegetable' and bug for 'virus/disease'. However, a couple of the more journalistic expressions also convey a sense of informality – namely, rocketing and shot up for 'rose/increased'.

There are no instances of contraction, ellipsis or dialectal expressions.

Text 6

This text contains no colloquial expressions, contractions, ellipses or dialectical expressions.

Based on these findings, we can argue that Text 4 and Text 5A both indicate or imply some degree of social contact between the communicative participants – some degree of familiarity or friendliness – while the relationship implied by Text 6 is one of social distance – no familiarity, friendliness or intimacy.

Such findings are relatively easy to explain with respect to Text 4 and Text 6.

Text 4 is a face-to-face conversation in which one speaker (Speaker 1) invites his/her respondents to discuss their own everyday, personal experiences. The sense of contact or closeness thus derives both from the casual, relaxed nature of the setting and the fact that the interlocutors are in direct face-to-face contact. It should be noted, however, that the colloquial expressions are not as frequent as they might be and that there are no actual instances of slang terms. Also the contractions are not as extensive as they might have been and there are few fully-fledged ellipses of clausal elements. This might be taken as evidence that, while the interlocutors are on *relatively* friendly terms, theirs is not the maximal closeness or intimacy which might be encountered had they been family members or very close friends.

The social distance of Text 6 follows naturally from the facts that (a) there is no real relationship between the writer and his/her audience, since it is written for a mass, essentially unknown, readership, and (b) the conventions of this domain of scientific research are such that a writer's style should be impersonal and 'objective', and should not engage in any way with the intended audience.

In contrast, the implication of some degree of social contact in Text 5A is slightly more problematic. Clearly this text is like Text 6 in that here, too, there is no actual relationship between writer and reader, apart from that which might result from their living in the same community and hence sharing some common experiences. Thus the journalist writes for a mass, unknown audience. Yet there are at least a few instances of language which would be expected only in contexts where there is some degree of familiarity or personal contact between interlocutors. This phenomenon has been noted by a number of writers on journalistic discourse and has been given the label **synthetic personalisation**. The effect is to simulate some degree of closeness between the newspaper and its readership, to imply that they are on familiar or friendly terms. This suggests to the readers of the newspaper that the journalistic authors are 'on the reader's own level' and hence forges, at least potentially, a bond between the reader and his/her newspaper. This approach is presumably seen by the managements of the newspapers which adopt this style (typically the tabloids) as appropriate for the newspaper's intended audience and as increasing its circulation.

In this section we have explored how it is possible to relate patterns in the use of particular words, phrases and structures to a text's tenor – that is, to the social roles and relationships of those involved in the communication. Specifically we have seen how particular lexical and grammatical features can be related to relative social status and to social distance. Yet this is by no means the full picture with regard to tenor.

Further issues relating to this interpersonal aspect of language will be explored in later units, especially Units 10 and 12.

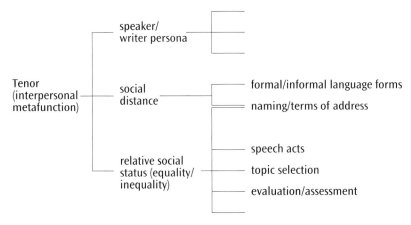

Figure 1 Map of tenor

③ LINGUISTIC INDICATORS OF FIELD – THE EXPERIENTIAL

We turn now to the second linguistically-significant aspect of a text's context of use – what is termed its field. Remember that this term refers to the domain of experience with which the text is concerned or which it represents. We are concerned with its subject matter, with the nature of the events, and with the entities or the state of affairs which it depicts.

3.1 Semantic domain

One indicator of a text's field is relatively straightforward when it comes to linguistic analysis. The subject matter (or matters) with which the text is concerned, known often as the semantic domain, can usually be identified by the relatively simple means of organising the text's nouns and verbs (and sometimes adjectives and adverbs) into the different topic and subtopic areas from which they are drawn.

We will begin by considering what we can say about the subject matter of our three main texts (Texts 4, 5A and 6, on pp. 18–19, 23–24 and 28–29 respectively) by identifying the various subject areas to which they refer and by considering what types of actions, events, objects, artefacts, people and other entities they deal with. Obviously the texts do have a common subject matter – this is one of the reasons they were selected for comparative analysis. They all contain vocabulary items which refer to human health and medicine, and to disease and its treatment. However, for the purposes of developing a systematic linguistic analysis, we want (a) to show this explicitly, and (b) to explore what differences there might be between the texts in terms of how they deal with this subject area and in terms of additional topic areas which might be included. In order to do this we will conduct the following analysis.

A CTIVITY 5 (allow about 20 minutes)

Fill in the following table, identifying vocabulary items from the three texts which refer to the topics listed.

See 'Answer to the activity' for feedback.

Topic	Text 4	Text 5A	Text 6
Diseases/injuries, symptoms/effects of disease/injury			
Medicines or other forms of treatment; actions/effects of treatments			
Parts or processes of the human body			
Health-care professionals and organisations/places of treatment			

COMMENT

The analysis provides clear support for our initial impressions – there are obvious similarities in subject matter in that all three texts include vocabulary which refers to (a) diseases/injuries, (b) treatments of these diseases/injuries, and (d) the people and/or institutions involved in this treatment. We can therefore say that the fields of the three texts are similar, to the extent that the texts all relate in some way to health care or 'medical treatment'. But the analysis also reveals that this similarity only holds at a relatively general level of meaning. When we look more closely at the various health-related meanings in the three texts we immediately discern some important differences.

3.2 Specialisation and assumptions of expert knowledge

Perhaps the most obvious of these differences relates to the question of whether the speaker/writer assumes that they share with the audience/addressee some specialist or expert knowledge – that is, some knowledge which an average adult member of the community would not possess. This is not simply a matter of whether the vocabulary refers to some technical or otherwise specialist field, since there are certain vocabulary items which have technical meanings but which would nevertheless be very widely known in the general community. Thus terms such as 'CD-ROM' or 'DVD' once started out as specialist (and they still refer to a technical area), and yet they have now become so widely used in everyday language that their use no longer implies an expert's knowledge. Similarly, from the technical fields of science and medicine we find terms such as 'X-ray', 'nuclear reactor' and 'HIV' which, though initially specialist, have now become part of everyday language.

The differences between the texts in terms of this assumption of shared specialist knowledge are relatively obvious. Nevertheless, it is still useful to conduct a systematic analysis by identifying and listing any such specialist terms (vocabulary that assumes a knowledge which would only be possessed by experts in a given field) in the three extracts.

◢ A CTIVITY 6 (allow about 15 minutes)

Use a table like the one below to list the specialist terms in Texts 4, 5A and 6 (on pp. 18–19, 23–24 and 28–29 respectively). You may want to make a special note of any items which you feel may pose problems for such a classification.

Text 4	Text 5A	Text 6

COMMENT

Your findings may well have demonstrated that Text 6 can be clearly distinguished from Texts 4 and 5A in terms of this notion of 'specialisation' – this is on the basis of the frequency with which Text 6 includes vocabulary which assumes expert knowledge. For example:

physiologic

ductal epithelium

estrogen receptor

receptor conformation

coregulatory proteins

antiestrogenic activity

ER-positive metastatic

ductal carcinoma-in-situ

Text 5A, in contrast, contains only one term that might potentially be seen as indicating such expert knowledge, the acronym *SARS*. Note, however, that a definition of the term is provided by means of the full form of the acronym, *severe acute respiratory syndrome*, with that definition provided quite early in the article. By giving such a full-form definition, the writer indicates that he/she does not assume a full knowledge of the term on the part of the reader. Note as well that at the time the report was published (in April 2003) SARS was very much under the media spotlight, with newspapers giving it very extensive coverage and with reports of the spread of the disease appearing nightly on television news bulletins. As a result of this coverage, the term had, at least partially, moved from being a specialist to being an everyday term, the meaning of which would be known to the average member of the community.

We can conclude that there is an important difference between Texts 6 and 5A with respect to field. Although both texts are concerned with disease and its treatment, they are concerned with very different contexts for that treatment and with very different ways of thinking about medical treatment. For Text 6, medical treatment is an expert field, an aspect of experience where specialist knowledge not possessed by the general public is assumed. For Text 5A, medical treatment is something which can still be understood by means of everyday notions and categories: it is an area of activity that can be depicted without recourse to specialist knowledge.

Text 4 is similar to Text 5A in that it does not contain the same high frequency of specialist terms that is found in Text 6. There are only four instances of words which might potentially be seen as assuming a particular expert knowledge. They are:

antibiotics

radiotherapy

biopsy

radiation.

Two of these – *antibiotics* and *radiation* – are in general currency in the wider speech community and hence should not be analysed as assuming expert knowledge. In contrast, *radiotherapy* and *biopsy* do seem to be more narrowly specialist, though clearly not to the same degree of specialisation as terms such as *epithelium* or *metastatic*. Of course, to reach more definitive conclusions (if, for example, investigating such specialisation for an essay or for publication in a research paper) we would almost certainly need to test such personal impressions in a more scientific manner. We might, for example, carry out a survey of a suitably large and diverse group of speakers, investigating whether they were familiar with such words and whether or not they could provide a rough definition for them. Similarly, we might make use of corpora of appropriate texts: if we found that a term occurred quite frequently and without definition in a corpus of journalistic texts aimed at a general readership, we could plausibly conclude that such a term was not specialist. Thus we find that the term *antibiotics* occurs 154 times, typically without definition, in a corpus of all the British tabloid newspapers from the three months from February to April 2003, indicating that it is in quite wide circulation. In contrast, the term *biopsy* only occurs 25 times in the same corpus, typically either only in special health sections within these newspapers or with a definition (for example: *I had a liver biopsy – removing a sample of tissue by syringe ...* (*The Daily Mail*, 15 April 2003)). This lends support to the conclusion that *biopsy* is less widely used than *antibiotic* and hence that its meaning may not generally be known. Not surprisingly, there are no instances of terms such as *epithelium* or *metastatic* in the same corpus. We might also make use of dictionaries which provide indicators of whether words are specialist or non-specialist.

In conclusion, we can say that both Texts 4 and 5A (conversation and news) are revealed as operating in fields where there is little or no assumption of specialist expertise. The worlds they refer to are those of everyday experience. In contrast, the field of Text 6 (medical science) is one where there are very clear assumptions of specialist expertise and hence the text operates in a domain of experience which is not everyday.

In the case of these particular texts, such findings probably seemed predictable, even obvious. However, if you have an interest in, or conduct research in, scientific or technological language, you will find that the situation regarding specialisation is not always so straightforward or clear-cut. Accordingly the usefulness of such an analytical framework is revealed. Scientific textbooks and texts which seek to popularise scientific or technological knowledge for mass audiences are particularly interesting in this regard. There you will find some often subtle graduations in specialisation.

This section has introduced two aspects of field. Other aspects will be addressed in later units, especially Units 11 and 13.

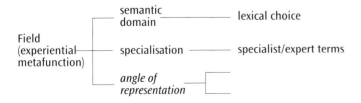

Figure 2 Map of field (italics indicate an aspect of field to be introduced later in the course)

◆4 LINGUISTIC INDICATORS OF MODE – THE TEXTUAL

We turn finally to the issue of the mode of a text and its linguistic indicators. Remember that in terms of mode we are interested in the nature of the text as a communicative event or action, in how it is produced and transmitted, in how it is organised internally as an unfolding sequence of meanings, and in how it relates to the context in which it is created or to the information it presents. Indicators of mode have already been discussed in some detail in earlier units, and later units will return to this topic. For the purposes of the current unit we will confine ourselves to demonstrating just a couple of key indicators.

4.1 Interactivity

The aspect of a text's mode which perhaps has the most obvious influence on the style of language is its **interactivity**. Here we are concerned with the following types of questions: was it constructed through a process of interaction between multiple interlocutors or non-interactively by one writer or speaker in isolation? If it was constructed interactively, what was the nature of this interaction? For example, were those involved in immediate face-to-face contact, as in the case of typical conversations, or was the contact oral/aural, as in the case of a telephone call?

In many cases, whether or not the text is interactive or non-interactive will be obvious. Clearly, interactive texts involve turn-taking, questions and answers, interruptions, overlaps, hesitators, and indicators of sympathetic support (for example, *right*, *OK*, *yep*, *really*). Non-interactive texts do not.

This variation is very simply demonstrated by our three primary texts. Text 4 includes many interactive elements – for example, the sequence of question and answer as speakers exchange turns; interruptions and overlaps as the exchange of turns is negotiated; supportive feedback insertions on the part of Speaker 1 as he/she encourages the interviewees to continue their accounts. Predictably, the two written texts are entirely without such indicators of interactivity.

However, it needs to be noted that the situation is by no means always this straightforward. Consider, as a brief example, the following extract from an article in a popular computing magazine. It is written and hence, presumably, non-interactive.

COMPUTERS get blamed for a lot of things. Whether it's a stock market crash, our children getting fatter or the decline in the state of the Top 40, you can bet it's all the fault of the PC. Sure, we all know computers are bad for us, but just how much damage can they do to this delicate wetware of flesh, bones and organs we all call home?

(Grittins, *PC Basics*, December 1998, p. 30)

We notice here a number of what appear to be more interactive elements, for example, the writer's apparently direct address to the audience (*you can bet ...*), the use of a question (*just how much damage can they do...?*) and what appears to be a response to some contribution from another speaker/writer (*Sure, we all know ...*). We shall consider what is going on here communicatively in later units. For now it is enough to note that the interactive versus non-interactive divide may not be as clear-cut as our earlier discussion may have suggested. And there are further questions arising from differences in the type of interactivity. For example, might we expect, and do we observe, systematic differences in face-to-face as opposed to telephone conversations? And what about the new types of interactive texts made possible by technological innovations, such as those which occur in written form in online chat rooms or bulletin boards? To what degree are these similar to, or different from, spoken interactions?

4.2 Spontaneity

A second key aspect of mode is that of **spontaneity.** Here we are concerned with whether the text was produced 'on-the-spot', that is, spontaneously and without the opportunity for pre-editing or correction (as is typically the case in casual conversation) or whether it was produced non-spontaneously, using a process by which it was possible to edit and correct the text (as is the case with much written language).

Some indicators of spontaneity are relatively obvious – for example, pauses, mid-utterance corrections or reformulations, repetitions, abrupt topic changes. Other indicators are less obvious. For example, research has discovered that there is a close correlation between the spontaneity/ non-spontaneity of a text's production and the density with which the text packages its information. High densities of information are associated with non-spontaneous production, with what is sometimes termed 'off-line' production. Lower densities are associated with spontaneous, 'on-the-fly', production, with what is sometimes termed 'online' or 'real-time' production.

◆ **A** **CTIVITY 7** (allow about 30 minutes)

Lexical density is one primary determiner of density of informational packaging (you may remember that this notion was introduced and explained in Unit 2 of Book 1). Accordingly, we will investigate lexical density in our three primary texts. For the purpose of this exercise we will confine the analysis to around 120 words from each text.

Calculate the lexical densities of the extracts overleaf. After you have completed the calculation, think about what your findings indicate with respect to the notion of spontaneity? Are there any problems in applying such a notion to describing the mode of these texts?

Remember that, to calculate lexical density, you count all lexical/ content words – nouns, adjectives, adverbs and lexical verbs (excluding the auxiliaries such as *is, was, will, must, should*). Then calculate this number as a percentage of the total number of words.

Text 7

I had skin cancer. I'd been digging in the garden and and I don't know whether I scratched myself with a ... 'cos I was doing my ... I don't whether a s+ a thorn caught me on the nose and then I'd been digging.

Cats and all sorts had been digging about, I hate cats, and it wouldn't heal up and it was going on and I was getting cream cream on my nose - it never ha+ healed up you see. So I went to the doctor's and they looked at it down the infirmary. Then they had to have those all these specialists round you you know and I thought, Why the heck am I seeing other people.

(118 words)

(Collins Cobuild Bank of English: subcorpus = brspok/UK)

Text 8

SALES of turnips are rocketing in China because the veg is said to cure SARS.

They are used in herbal remedies sold to treat severe acute respiratory syndrome.

Wholesale prices of turnips in China's capital Beijing have shot up THIRTY PER CENT in a week amid fears over the deadly flu-like virus. Carrots, garlic and ginger are also included in the potions and shops have been selling out.

The global death toll from SARS rose to 153 yesterday. Nine were reported in Hong Kong – the most in one day there so far. They included a woman aged 34, who died while giving birth. The condition of the baby was not known.

China has been hit hardest by SARS, with 64 deaths.

(121 words)

(Adapted from Russell, *The Sun*, 16 April 2003)

Text 9

The sex hormone estrogen is important for many physiologic processes. Prolonged stimulation of breast ductal epithelium by estrogen, however, can contribute to the development and progression of breast cancer, and treatments designed to block estrogen's effects are important options in the clinic. Tamoxifen and other similar drugs are effective in breast cancer prevention and treatment by inhibiting the proliferative effects of estrogen that are mediated through the estrogen receptor (ER). However, these drugs also have many estrogenic effects depending on the tissue and gene, and they are more appropriately called selective estrogen receptor modulators (SERMs). SERMs bind ER, alter receptor conformation, and facilitate binding of coregulatory proteins that activate or repress transcriptional activation of estrogen target genes.

(117 words)

(Osborne et al., 2000, pp. 3172–86; quoted in PubMed website, 4 September 2003)

COMMENT

In the following analyses we have underlined all lexical words (nouns, adjectives, adverbs and lexical verbs).

Text 7

I had skin cancer. I'd been digging in the garden and and I don't know whether I scratched myself with a 'cos I was doing my I don't whether a s+ a thorn caught me on the nose and then I'd been digging

Cats and all sorts had been digging about, I hate cats, and it wouldn't heal up and it was going on and I was getting cream cream on my nose - it never ha+ healed up you see. So I went to the doctor's and they looked at it down the infirmary. Then they had to have those all these specialists round you you know and I thought, Why the heck am I seeing other people.

Lexical density = (35 lexical words ÷ 118 words) × 100 = 30%

Text 8

SALES of turnips are rocketing in China because the veg is said to cure SARS.

They are used in herbal remedies sold to treat severe acute respiratory syndrome.

Wholesale prices of turnips in China's capital Beijing have shot up THIRTY PER CENT in a week amid fears over the deadly flu-like virus. Carrots, garlic and ginger are also included in the potions and shops have been selling out.

The global death toll from SARS rose to 153 yesterday. Nine were reported in Hong Kong – the most in one day there so far. They included a woman aged 34, who died while giving birth. The condition of the baby was not known.

China has been hit hardest by SARS, with 64 deaths.

Lexical density = (64 lexical words ÷ 121 words) × 100 = 53%

You will notice here that numbers have been classified as function words. This is because they are a type of determiner.

Text 9

The sex hormone estrogen is important for many physiologic processes. Prolonged stimulation of breast ductal epithelium by estrogen, however, can contribute to the development and progression of breast cancer, and treatments designed to block estrogen's effects are important options in the clinic. Tamoxifen and other similar drugs are effective in breast cancer prevention and treatment by inhibiting the proliferative effects of estrogen that are mediated through the estrogen receptor (ER). However, these drugs also have many estrogenic effects depending on the tissue and gene, and they are more appropriately called selective estrogen receptor modulators (SERMs). SERMs bind ER, alter receptor conformation, and facilitate binding of coregulatory proteins that activate or repress transcriptional activation of estrogen target genes.

Lexical density = (75 lexical words ÷ 117 words) × 100 = 64%

This lexical density analysis very clearly separates the conversational text (Text 7) from the two written texts (Texts 8 and 9), indicating that in this case lexical density is a good indicator of online/offline production, and hence of one key aspect of mode.

There is just one area of complication. How do we account for the difference in lexical densities of the two written texts (53% versus 64%)? Clearly there is no proposal here that non-spontaneous/offline production necessarily always results in exactly the same lexical density. Obviously there are other factors which also have a role in determining the final density of informational packaging. One factor may be a feeling in the writer that less densely packed texts are easier to read/comprehend. So, in this case, the lower lexical density of the news text may result from some effort on the part of the journalist to ensure that his text is relatively easy to comprehend for a general readership.

Further aspects of mode will be covered in later units, especially Units 9, 14, 15 and 16.

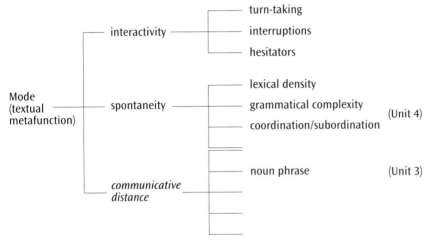

Figure 3 Map of mode (italics indicate an aspect of mode to be introduced later in the course)

⑤ INSIGHTS FROM A LONGMAN-STYLE CORPUS APPROACH

A CTIVITY 8 (allow about two hours)

Read Chapter 3, 'Corpus-Based Comparisons of Registers' by Douglas Biber and Susan Conrad in the course reader, *Applying English Grammar*.

The research and discussion set out in the reading provide an alternative, though complementary, perspective to that given in this unit. Our concern in the unit has been with accounting for the register of individual texts (their grammatical style) by reference to certain key aspects of those texts' context of use – namely, their tenor, field and mode. We have been interested in the distinctive or characteristic linguistic features of individual texts by which we might first identify, and then compare and contrast, different linguistic registers.

Biber and Conrad are also interested in the issue of register and hence in the lexicogrammatical variation which can be observed in language drawn from different social contexts. However, their concerns and objectives are somewhat different from those which have directed the unit up to this point. They are interested in register as it operates in the very broadest sense: their orientation is not towards the analysis of individual texts and small groupings of texts. Rather, their primary interest is in discovering whether the frequency of particular lexical and grammatical elements varies across the language used in different social settings. For this reason, they construct large multi-million-word repositories of language, with each repository (or corpus) containing many texts drawn from a particular social situation. Specifically, they construct four repositories of language by collecting texts from the social situations of conversation, fiction, news and academic research.

What this means is that each of these repositories (or corpora) is likely to contain texts which are quite diverse in their style and in their communicative objectives. For example, Biber and Conrad's news corpus includes hard news reports, editorials, commentaries, letters to the editor and arts reviews. Such different text types are obviously highly likely to be different in at least some important aspects of grammatical style, a point which was demonstrated above when we compared the news report text (Text 5A) with the editorial (Text 5B). Similarly, the grouping of academic prose includes texts from very different disciplines, for example, from the 'hard' sciences, the social sciences and the humanities. Here, once again we would expect to find some very marked differences in style and perhaps in communicative objectives as well.

What this means is that the approach to exploring linguistic variation which we demonstrated above and that set out by Biber and Conrad are each designed to address somewhat different questions. The approach which we set out is appropriate for investigating the style of individual texts and small groupings of texts, while Biber and Conrad's is appropriate for investigating large-scale patterns of grammatical variability across large groupings of texts. Which approach you employ will depend on the nature of your research project and the types of questions you are seeking to answer. (Of course, it is still possible that in large-scale projects you may want to employ both approaches in order to investigate different aspects of the issues you are addressing.)

To summarise: Biber and Conrad (and *The Longman Grammar of Spoken and Written English* (Biber et al., 1999)) use the term 'register' in a slightly different way from the way in which it is used within SFL (as outlined in Section 1 of this unit). Biber and Conrad use what we call in this course Longman registers – the Longman registers of academic prose, conversation, news and fiction – as a general term to identify very broad-based differences in the use of language. In contrast, within SFL it is used to identify smaller-scale differences in style at the level of individual texts and relatively small groupings of texts.

A CTIVITY 9 (allow about 10 minutes)

In the reading you will have observed that the authors report findings with respect to the use of personal pronouns across the Longman registers. In particular they report findings which show that personal pronouns occur with a high frequency in conversation but with a much lower frequency in news. When we calculate the frequency of personal pronouns in our conversational text (Text 4, pp. 18–19) and in our news text (Text 5A, pp. 23–24) we produce a similar finding – Text 4 has a high frequency of personal pronouns and Text 5A a very low frequency.

Biber and Conrad propose an explanation of why personal pronouns are generally frequent in conversation and significantly less frequent in news. Do you think this explanation also applies in the case of our conversational text (Text 4) and our news text (Text 5A)? (You might like to write a brief answer in your notebook.)

What sort of conclusions can we draw from the fact that the findings for our individual conversational and news texts are in line with the findings for Biber and Conrad's conversational and news corpora? Can we, for example, conclude that our texts are in some way typical examples of conversation and news in this regard?

COMMENT

Biber and Conrad propose that pronouns occur frequently in conversation because speakers in this mode typically focus on personal information and feelings, and hence make repeated use of the pronoun *I*. Also, conversation is directly interactive and so it frequently uses the pronoun *you*. There is also a shared situation, so speakers can refer to that situation with third-person pronouns without being explicit about the intended meaning. Since news reports do not usually focus to the same degree on personal information, are not interactive and do not involve a shared immediate physical setting, they make considerably less use of pronouns.

In this case, the explanation which applies to Biber and Conrad's corpora also seems to apply to our individual texts. Clearly the main speaker in our individual conversational text was concerned to project her own personality, to indicate her personal role in what is being described and to express opinions. Accordingly the personal pronoun *I* occurred frequently. Also, the text involved interaction and therefore the interactive pronoun *you* occurred frequently. The low frequency of personal pronouns in our news text can be similarly accounted for. The low incidence of *I* results from the fact that the writers of such reports typically remain anonymous – that they do not seek to reveal their own subjective role in the communication. The lower incidence of *you* results from the non-interactive nature of such texts.

It may be tempting, therefore, to conclude that this provides definitive evidence that our individual texts are in fact typical examples of conversational and news language, at least with regard to their use of personal pronouns. Certainly the fact that the figures for our individual texts are similar to the figures for Biber and Conrad's large collections of texts would justify us in proposing this as a working hypothesis. It is, however, a hypothesis which would require further investigation and testing. We would need to investigate, for example, whether all the texts in Biber and Conrad's news corpus feature this low proportion of personal pronouns or whether their final figure for pronouns was arrived at by a process of averaging out. That is, we would need to investigate whether the frequency of personal pronouns in their news texts stayed at essentially the same level across all their texts or whether it fluctuated significantly, with some having significantly higher numbers and others significantly lower numbers. We might also assemble our own corpus of news or of conversational texts and seek to discover whether pronoun frequencies fluctuate or remain stable across those texts. In this regard note that our second news text (Text 5B, pp. 24–25) contains many more first and second person forms (pronouns and possessive determiners) than our main news text (Text 5A, pp. 23–24). While 5A contains just the one instance of such a form (*our* in *Manager Thomas Laue said: 'It will be our share in controlling this plague.'*), 5B contains eight instances (four of *our*, one of *ourselves*, two of *we* and one of *let's*).

ACTIVITIES **CD-ROM**   (allow about two hours)

Now work through the activities for this unit on the Activities CD-ROM.

CONCORDANCER AND **C**ORPUS **CD-ROM**

(allow about three hours)

Read the 'Introduction to Book 2' in the *Corpus Tasks* booklet. Next work through the tasks for this unit on the Concordancer and Corpus CD-ROM using the *Corpus Tasks* booklet.

Conclusion

In this unit we have investigated a framework by which it is possible to systematically relate the style of a text to the social context in which that text operates. By this means we identify and compare what are termed different 'registers' of language. Specifically we have explored how social roles and relationships (tenor), subject matter (field) and the nature of the text as a communicative event (mode) influence particular aspects of grammar and vocabulary. We have seen how these different aspects of social situation are typically reflected in particular lexicogrammatical elements: field is reflected in experiential aspects of the language, tenor in interpersonal aspects and mode in textual aspects. We have shown how it is possible to explain particular grammatical features in a text by reference to the communicative functions these features serve in a particular context of use. In this way, we develop a better understanding of the distinctive stylistic properties of different text types and are able to provide systematic explanations of stylistic differences between different text types. The table overleaf provides an overview of this analytical framework. When we use this approach to analyse a text, we are carrying out a **register analysis**.

Our exposition has only provided an introduction to the topic of how language use reflects and is determined by its context of use. We have demonstrated the general principles at work but we have by no means presented a full account of all the ways in which tenor, field and mode determine grammatical style. The account which was begun here will be extended and deepened in later units.

Learning outcomes

After completing Unit 8, you should have developed your knowledge and understanding of the concept of register. In addition, you should be familiar with the idea of field, tenor and mode, as well as the metafunctions (experiential, interpersonal and textual).

You should have developed your ability to:
◆ *describe* grammatical features in a text
◆ *interpret* texts and their grammatical features in relation to their situations of use.

Scheme for register analysis

Aspects of situation	Linguistic functions (shown by grammatical features)
Field Subject matter/associated activity/ domain of experience:	Experiential: representation of experience; categorisation and other structuring (shown through e.g. lexis, transitivity, types of processes, participants and circumstances):
Tenor Equality/inequality: Social distance: Speaker/writer persona:	Interpersonal: expression of roles, purposes and attitudes; linguistic construction of addressee and addressor (shown through e.g. pronouns, modality, evaluative language, speech acts and formal/colloquial/technical vocabulary):
Mode Channel (speech vs. print): Spontaneity of production: Possibility of feedback:	Textual: construction of text as medium; its organisation; cohesion; foregrounding; emphasis (shown through e.g. lexical density, markers of interaction and themes):

Key terms introduced and revisited	
context of use	relative social status
experiential metafunction [ideational]	semantic domain
field, tenor and mode	social distance
interactivity	speaker/writer persona
interpersonal metafunction	spontaneity
Longman register	synthetic personalisation
register	systemic functional linguistics (SFL)
register analysis	textual metafunction

Near equivalents are given in [ ].

Answer to the activity

ACTIVITY 5

Topic	Text 4	Text 5A	Text 6

Diseases/injuries or symptoms/ effects of disease/injury	flu
	lump
	cancer
	scratched
	sick
		SARS
		bug
		SARS
		severe acute respiratory
		  syndrome
		flu
		virus
		SARS
		SARS
		Infected
		SARS
		infected
		virus
		SARS
		plague
		SARS
		symptoms
		illness
		ill
		SARS
		SARS
		epidemic
		bug
			breast cancer
			breast cancer
			osteoporosis
			estrogen-regulated
			  malignancies
			ER-positive metastatic
			  breast cancer
			ductal carcinoma-in-situ
			breast cancer

Medicines or other forms of treatments; actions/effects of treatments	jabs antibiotics antibiotics cream radiotherapy biopsy cut out stitch radiation	CURE cure remedies potions Caesarean section remedy cure high-speed test treated surgical masks	treatments Tamoxifen drugs drugs selective estrogen receptor modulators SERMs SERMs SERMs SERMs estrogenic effects agonist activity antiestrogenic activity

			functional activities
			treatment
			prevention
			treatment
			prevention
			SERMs
			hormone replacement therapy
			Tamoxifen
			tamoxifen
Parts or processes of the human body	neck		sex hormone estrogen
	skin		physiologic processes
	nose		breast ductal epithelium
	heal		estrogen
	nose		estrogen's
	healed		estrogen
	nose		estrogen receptor tissue
	eyes		gene
			estrogen receptor modulators
			ER
			receptor conformation
			coregulatory proteins
			transcriptional activation
			estrogen target genes
Health-care professionals and organisations/places of treatment	doctor	laboratories	clinic
	doctor's	hospital	
	infirmary	hospice	
	specialists	hospital	
	infirmary	World Health Organisation	

Unit 9

Packaging and staging information

Prepared for the course team by Kieran O'Halloran and Caroline Coffin

CONTENTS

Materials required

While studying this unit, you will need:

the course reader

the Activities CD-ROM.

Knowledge assumed

You should be familiar with the following before starting this unit:

classifier

collocation

describer

determiner

head

nominalisation

numerative

qualifier

rank scale.

Introduction

You are going to read the same information in two news texts (Texts 1 and 2). Which news text do you prefer and why?

Text 1

It has recently been discovered that turnips can 'cure' SARS. People are increasingly demanding vegetables in the scare surrounding the SARS disease which is killing many people. People are demanding turnips because some people say that eating turnips cures SARS.

Text 2

TURNIPS 'CURE SARS'

Demand for veg rockets in killer bug scare

SALES of turnips are rocketing in China because the veg is said to cure SARS.

(Russell, *The Sun*, 16 April 2003)

You probably think the second one works better because it presents the information more effectively – something to do with the way the information is 'wrapped'. By way of an analogy, think about the shape of Coca-Cola bottles and how it makes what is inside them more interesting. Coca-Cola bottles have sleek curves – the Coca-Cola inside is framed in an aesthetically-pleasing way. We can connect physically with the bottle as well – it fits nicely into a palm of a hand. But pour lots of Coca-Cola into a bucket, and then offer glasses of it to your friends – they will probably not 'connect' with it in the same way and may refuse to drink it.

The first text has a similar effect – it is as though the information has spilled out of its packaging, making it less readily engaging. Little thought has been given to how to frame the information in an interesting way, how to stage it to reduce the repetition. Our attention is not captured and so the text lacks impact. All these things – lack of packaging, staging and thus impact – are certainly true of the first text. But say you were teaching a novice news writer to write punchy news text (like the second) and they produced the first text. Do you think saying to them that their effort lacked impact because of an absence of information staging and packaging would help this novice to rectify things immediately? Think how much more quickly you would be able to teach him or her if you both shared the same resources for grammatically describing what is wrong with the first text and what is right with the second text. You would be able to translate 'lack of packaging, staging and thus impact' into precise and concrete advice for the novice news writer which would, as a result, be far more helpful.

This unit will give you the skills to analyse and articulate the packaging and staging of information in texts, things which are important for making your writing engaging and coherent. It will also enhance and extend your descriptive and interpretative skills in examining text as well as your critical evaluative skills in helping you to say precisely why a piece of text does not work. Such a precise set of descriptive, interpretative and critically-evaluative tools will enable you to examine keenly your own writing and so improve your ability to communicate effectively. In Unit 8 you saw how academic text, conversation and news text differ from one another. In this unit we shall be looking again at texts from the Longman registers, including fiction, to understand how users of English package and stage information so as to produce effective English and thus to avoid the kind of writing in Text 1.

In Unit 8 you were introduced to a framework for exploring English grammar in context. In that unit you saw that linked to the contextual domain of field is a range of grammatical resources for representing human experience in terms of happenings, the participants involved in the happenings and the circumstances surrounding them. You also saw that, linked to tenor, there is a set of resources for building social relations and enabling speakers to enter into different types of interaction and to express and negotiate with different points of view. Finally, you were introduced to an area of English grammar related to the contextual domain of mode. This area of grammar helps speakers to package and organise information and to produce and transmit texts using a wide range of media, such as the telephone, email and television. Mode is the focus of this unit.

 PACKAGING INFORMATION: ROLE OF THE NOUN PHRASE

In Book 1 Unit 4 we looked at how the noun phrase can be carved up into a set of functional elements which each serve to capture a different dimension of the head noun. We saw that the elements referred to as determiners, numeratives and describers (also called epithets) precede the head noun (and hence are premodifiers) whereas qualifiers (postmodifiers) follow it. As revision, complete the next activity before we explore the structure of premodifiers in more detail.

◆ A CTIVITY 1 (allow about 20 minutes)

Look at the following opening paragraph of the novel *The Sea, The Sea* and observe how the writer, Iris Murdoch, builds up the setting for her story through the resources of the noun phrase. Use the table overleaf to analyse the noun phrases, some of which have already been completed as examples.

See 'Answers to the activities' for feedback.

> The sea which lies before me as I write glows rather than sparkles in the bland May sunshine. With the tide turning, it leans quietly against the land, almost unflecked by ripples or by foam. Near to the horizon it is a luxurious purple, spotted with regular lines of emerald green. At the horizon it is indigo. Near to the shore, where my view is framed by rising heaps of humpy yellow rock, there is a band of lighter green, icy and pure, less radiant, opaque however, not transparent. We are in the north, and the bright sunshine cannot penetrate the sea. Where the gentle water taps the rocks there is still a surface skin of colour. The cloudless sky is very pale at the indigo horizon which it lightly pencils in with silver. Its blue gains towards the zenith and vibrates there. But the sky looks cold, even the sun looks cold.
>
> (Murdoch, 1978, p. 1)

Determiner (pointing words)	Numerative (quantity)	Describer	Classifier	Head	Qualifier (long describer)
				sunshine	
		luxurious		purple *	
				lines	
	rising (*describer*) heaps of	humpy yellow		rock	
a				band	of lighter green, icy and pure, less radiant, *opaque however, not transparent
				sunshine	
				water	
				skin	
				sky	
				horizon	

* Literary styles of writing sometimes create interesting questions for grammatical description and interpretation. For example, in this passage, *purple* is used as a noun whereas typically it would be a describer. Likewise, in the noun phrase *a band of lighter green...* the use of ellipsis makes it difficult to tell which qualifiers belong to the head. For example, I could argue that there is ellipsis: *<It is> opaque however, not transparent.*

COMMENT

You may or may not like the literary style of Iris Murdoch but I think you would agree that in this opening paragraph the noun phrase serves as a resource for capturing both the look and feel of the landscape. The use of colour (*yellow, emerald green, lighter green*) and texture (*humpy, gentle*) in both the describers and qualifiers help the reader to imagine and enter into the scene that lies before the main protagonist, Charles Arrowby. In addition, the use of first-person perspective means that the reader is observing the scene from Charles Arrowby's point of view. Thus although the picture of the sea may seem somewhat overwrought, almost too painstakingly described, we need to take into account that this is the way Arrowby perceives the scene and thus from the beginning of the novel we have an insight into his thoughts and responses, his 'angle on the world'.

A CTIVITY 2 (allow about 10 minutes)

Now look at the following text, which again is the introduction to a novel and describes a scene. This time you will see that although there are many adjectives serving to capture the colours and atmosphere of Ayemenem, a town in India, the description seems clumsy. Can you diagnose what is wrong – grammatically speaking?

> May in Ayemenem is hot. May is also brooding. The days are long. They are humid. The river shrinks. The mango trees are still. The mango trees are also dust green. Black crows are on the mango trees. They gorge on the mangoes. The mangoes are bright. The bananas are red. The bananas ripen. There are jackfruits. The jackfruits burst. Bluebottles are dissolute. They hum vacuously in the air. The air is fruity. The bluebottles then stun themselves against windowpanes. These windowpanes are clear. The bluebottles die. When they die they are fatly baffled in the sun.
>
> The nights are clear. But the nights are suffused with sloth. The nights are also suffused with expectation. This expectation is sullen.

C O M M E N T

You will probably have worked out that nearly all the adjectives in the paragraph are functioning as complements or, from a functional point of view, as participants (see Book 1 Unit 3). Apart from *black* in *black crows*, none of them serve as describers in a noun phrase structure. The descriptions seem drawn out and stilted. They are a list of things that we might see in Ayemenem. But they have not been shaped and compacted in such a way as to capture our attention in writing.

So, if we were aspiring novelists (and some of you may be!) what could we do to improve these descriptions? How might noun phrases serve to capture our attention, to create a more eloquent and smoother unfolding of the scene?

By filling in the table overleaf you should be able to see that fiction writers can exploit the resource of the noun phrase. The scene above, for example, could be made more descriptively compact and therefore less drawn out. Use the table to build up the head nouns which we have extracted from the text. Think whether the adjectives in the original text would work better if they functioned as describers or qualifiers in noun phrases.

Describer	Classifier	Head	Qualifier
		May	
		mangoes	
		trees	
		bananas	
		bluebottles	
		air	
		windowpanes	
		expectation	

You may now be interested in turning to 'Answers to the activities' to see how Ayemenem was originally described by the Indian writer, Arundhati Roy. I think you will agree that the opening paragraph of her novel *The God of Small Things* was (before we tampered with it) a successful and imaginative evocation of a tropical and exotic landscape full of colour and life. Much of this seems to be a result of how she has exploited the resources of the noun phrase to realise compacted description which then focuses our attention. It is useful for us, as writers and speakers, to be consciously aware of how we have choices in the way we package information. Of course, the mode we are operating in will have an impact on what choices we make. For example, if we are chatting to a friend we are unlikely to fill our speech with densely packed noun phrases. On the other hand, if we are engaged in a piece of creative writing we might think long and hard about how best to organise our descriptions, for example, as participants in relational processes (*the trees are lush and green*) or as describers in noun phrases (*the lush, green trees*).

If we examine corpus evidence for fictional writing, not surprisingly we find that describers are used in noun phrases more extensively than in the other Longman registers (academic writing, news and conversation). The advantages of examining corpora is that we can also see what *types* of describers are the most common in fiction. This is something we cannot discern just from our own intuition. Have a look at the table opposite, from Biber et al. (1999, pp. 512–13), to see which describers are the most common in the fiction corpus.

You should be able to see that, in fiction, describers of colour, time, size and evaluation are common. Indeed, the range of describers in fiction is far greater than in any of the other Longman registers. You should also be able to see that classifiers are much less common in fiction. Clearly, classifiers do not provide the descriptive detail which is characteristic of fictional narrative.

Table 1

The most common adjectives used as describers and classifiers in noun phrases across Longman registers (all that occur more than 200 times per million words in at least one register); occurrences per million words

▢ over 500   ▪ over 200   ▯ over 80

Describers	CONV	FICT	NEWS	ACAD
Size / Amount				
big	▪	▪	▪	
little	▪	▪	▯	
long	▯	▪	▪	▯
small		▪	▪	▪
great		▪	▪	▪
high		▯	▪	▪
low		▯	▯	▯
large		▯	▯	▪
Time				
new	▪	▪	▢	▢
old	▪	▪	▢	▯
young		▪	▪	▯
Colour				
black	▯	▪	▯	
white	▯	▪	▯	
red		▪	▯	
dark		▪		
Evaluative				
good	▪	▪	▪	▪
best	▯	▯	▪	▯
right	▯	▯	▯	▯
nice	▪	▯		
important			▯	▪
special			▯	▪

Classifiers	CONV	FICT	NEWS	ACAD
Scope				
same	▪	▪	▪	▢
whole	▯	▪	▯	▪
different	▯	▯	▯	▢
full		▯	▪	▯
general			▪	▪
major			▪	
final			▪	▯
main			▯	
single			▯	▪
Topical				
political			▪	▪
public			▪	▪
social			▯	▢
human		▯		▪
international			▪	▯
national			▪	▯
economic			▯	▪

I am currently in a very different setting from that described by Roy. Right now, the English landscape looks rather drab and dull (particularly when compared to India) and it is May which, in the UK, far from being a hot and brooding month, can be a cool and variable time of the year – a mix of showers and sunshine. This is what the weather has been like outside my window, at least today. By drawing to some extent on the Longman corpus evidence, I will now try to build up this information as though I were writing a piece of fiction – that is, build up noun phrases with describers and qualifiers. As I look through my window, this is what I see through my 'fictional' eyes:

a black sky with big clouds, low and ominous

lush, green trees with the new leaves dancing in the wind

dark, red-brick Victorian terraced houses spattered with rain drops

a long street with litter drifting along the gutter

I am not going to be the twenty-first-century Charles Dickens so I shall leave my efforts at fiction there. In fact, I shall switch hats from novelist to meteorologist – someone who makes an academic study of the weather. If I had to report the weather with my meteorologist's hat on, I would not use so many describers. I would need to make more general claims about the weather so that such specific detail would be less relevant. So I would most probably package information with both describers *and* classifiers. I might use noun phrases such as:

High pollen count and low humidity. Variable wind at 3 mph.
Normal weather for this time of year.

In line with the Longman corpus evidence for academic prose, you will see that I have used the describers of size *high* and *low*. I have also used a scope classifier (see the table on the preceding page), *variable*, with a qualifier, *at 3 mph*. *Variable* is a scope classifier since, like other scope classifiers (such as *full*, etc., in the table), it tells you the extent to which something is the case. Notice how, in discussing wind, I am using classifiers instead of describers and my qualifier, *at 3 mph*, gives numerical information. Numerical information on wind speed applies generally; the effects of wind on the litter in my street is not generally relevant.

What about the conversational register? A friend of mine rang me up earlier to arrange a game of tennis on the courts near where I live. I checked the weather outside and I can definitely tell you I did not say: *I can see a black sky with big clouds, low and ominous*. If I had, my tennis partner might have thought I was pretentious, at the very least. And if I had moved into the academic register and said it would be difficult to play because of the *variable wind speed*, he might have thought I was trying to keep my distance. Besides, because I was talking on the phone,

I was producing language 'on the spot' and, as we noted in Unit 8, there is a close correlation between the spontaneity/non-spontaneity of a text's production and the density with which the text packages its information. So I used simple describers and simple noun phrases (indicated below with [ ]) such as:

Well, there's [a lot of wind]. I really don't think it's [a great day].

You will see that these describers indicate amount and evaluation respectively. They are also short adjectives. Indeed, as Biber et al. (1999, p. 513) say, describers in conversation in the Longman corpus are:

mostly monosyllabic and simple, consistent with the generally less-complex structures in this register. Semantically, most of these words characterize size, time, or personal evaluation.

Excessive description of the weather in conversation would be a strange thing. We do not normally spend a lot of time describing the weather to one another in conversation because we are not trying to establish a certain mood or effect. Most of the time we are more interested in whether or not the weather will impede our activities. My friend added disappointingly that he would have been taking his new tennis racket. But if he had started salivating with classifiers, describers and qualifiers to tell me

I have a new, German, titanium-based racket with a lightweight head

or

I'll be looking cool in my new, tight black Nike shorts with white piping

I would not have been impressed – just concerned.

I have been conveying the weather in the Longman registers of conversation, fiction and academic prose. Now to translate what is outside my window into the other Longman register – news. What is going on outside my window is hardly news, but what might it look like if I had to convey the scene in the news register? Unlike in fiction and conversation, classifiers and describers are both common in news, as you can see from the above corpus results table. I have mentioned a subcategory of classifier: 'scope'. You will see this in the table above another subcategory: 'topical' – this just refers to the subject matter of which the classifier is part. There is another subcategory of classifiers which is common in news but that is not in the table. This is what Biber et al. (1999, p. 513) call 'affiliatives' – i.e. where someone or something belongs. In the Longman corpus for news, common affiliative adjectives include *American, British, European, Scottish*. So in trying to translate my experience of the weather outside into news, I might arrive at something like the following (key noun phrases indicated with [ ]).

[British academic] Fergus O'Smith announced today from [his first-floor flat] that [the recent weather conditions in London] had been totally unacceptable – once again Britain had failed to match [the weather targets set by Spain]. Though he was reluctant to discuss [his personal circumstances], a spokesperson intimated that [the recent poor weather] had prevented him from playing [his favourite game] – tennis.

We have here the classifiers *British, weather, personal* as well as the describers *recent, poor, favourite*. Note the affiliative classifier *British*. We have been drawing on a rather detailed table of information. So that you can see the differences between the registers more clearly, let us zoom out from looking at examples of describers and classifiers and look at the frequency distribution for these categories. In doing so, you will be able to get a bird's-eye view of which types of describer and classifier are most or least common across the Longman registers. For instance, you will see clearly how affiliative describers are much less common in conversation and fiction than in news and academic prose.

Table 2

Bird's-eye view of common describers and classifiers

Occurrences per million words

Each ● represents 3 adjectives, each occurring at least 100 times

	CONV	FICT	NEWS	ACAD
Describers				
evaluative	●●	●●●●	●●●	●●●●
size	●	●●●●	●●●	●●●
time	●	●	●●●	
colour	●	●●●	●	
miscellaneous		●●●	●	●●
Classifiers				
scope	●	●●	●●●●●●	●●●●●●●●●●● ●●●●●●●●
topical/miscellaneous			●●●●●	●●●●●●●●●●
affiliative			●●●	●

(Biber et al., 1999, p. 511)

When we trialled this unit, we asked some of our 'guinea-pig' students who tested the course to construct noun phrases similar to the ones above, using the above Longman corpus evidence as a guide. That is, we asked them to describe their surroundings or what was going on in their lives in noun phrases with the different Longman register 'hats' on. Opposite we have a very successful set of descriptions written by one of the student testers, Judy Anderson. We also asked Judy for paragraphs of continuous prose which contain these noun phrases (as well as some others). The prose descriptions are included after each table. Notice how her use of describers, classifiers and qualifiers varies according to the Longman register.

Conversation (on telephone)

It's a hectic life here. I'm really busy with work deadlines but on Sunday we'll be packing our things, getting ready to fly off for a good holiday.

Conversation

determiner (pointing word)	numerative (quantity)	describer	classifier	head	qualifier (long describer)
a		hectic		life	
			work	deadlines	
our				things	
a		good		holiday	

News

British schoolgirl Jessica Anderson spoke out yesterday about the total failure of her mother to cook a proper supper. 'She blames the recent hot weather, saying it makes cooking over a hot stove a health hazard,' says the twelve-year-old bitterly.

A family spokesman blames unforeseen changes in the 40-year-old housewife's personal circumstances, saying he felt the issue should never have entered the public arena.

News

determiner (pointing word)	numerative (quantity)	describer	classifier	head	qualifier (long describer)
			British schoolgirl	Jessica Anderson	
the		total		failure	of her mother to cook a proper supper
the		recent hot		weather	
		unforeseen		changes	in the 40-year-old housewife's personal circumstances
the			public	arena	

Fiction

I sit at the table in the airless, hot kitchen, wondering what to write next. Monty, our large, black Labrador, sprawls sleeping at my feet in the darkness under the table, trying to keep cool. Outside the window, I see the dappled-green, inviting shade of the chestnut tree. Just beyond its reach, the sun-drenched roses are wilting in the heat. There's a sudden roar of a motorcycle driving too fast over the humps in the road outside. Then silence, only the gentle ticking of the kitchen clock.

Fiction

determiner (pointing word)	numerative (quantity)	describer	classifier	head	qualifier (long describer)
the		airless, hot		kitchen	
our		large, black		Labrador	
the				darkness	under the table
the		sun-drenched		roses	
the		dappled-green, inviting		shade	of the chestnut tree
a		sudden		roar	of a motorcycle driving too fast over the humps in the road outside
the		gentle		ticking	of the kitchen clock

Academic

The temperature in the kitchen is 10 degrees higher than the air outside. This has been caused by a combination of factors: sun streaming through the Velux window and the constant emission of heat from the Aga cooker. Lack of air circulation is another factor in the rise of temperature.

Academic prose

determiner (pointing word)	numerative (quantity)	describer	classifier	head	qualifier (long describer)
the				temperature	in the kitchen
a				combination	of factors
				sun	streaming through the Velux window
the		constant		emission	of heat from the Aga cooker
				lack	of air circulation
another				factor	in the rise of temperature

A CTIVITY 3 (allow about 40 minutes)

Wherever you are – and right now you may be in a garden or a public park, or travelling somewhere by train – I would like you to use the tables on the next page to build up some noun phrases that capture your surroundings just as our student tester, Judy, did. As above, you will see that the tables have the headings: conversation, fiction, news, academic prose. This is because I would like you to build up some noun phrases in the same way as was done above. That is, I want you to wear four different 'writing hats'. Convey your surroundings in noun phrases as though your were talking to a friend, say, on the phone; writing a piece of fiction and so conveying your surroundings in noun phrases to achieve a mood or effect; reporting your surroundings as though they were news; writing about your surroundings academically. Build up five different noun phrases for each Longman register. To guide you, use the Longman corpus data in Tables 1 and 2 and by all means use the most commmon describers, as indicated in Table 1. Use others as well if you want. But, above all, make sure you keep in line with the general pattern of describers across the registers. So, for example, use more describers than classifiers in fiction.

Once you have done this, construct a paragraph of continuous prose in the same way that Judy did. Alternatively, you may decide this activity is easier to complete by producing paragraphs of continuous prose first and then sifting through them for noun phrases and seeing ways of expanding them in a style suitable for the register. It is up to you how you approach the task.

Conversation

determiner (pointing word)	numerative (quantity)	describer	classifier	head	qualifier (long describer)

Fiction

determiner (pointing word)	numerative (quantity)	describer	classifier	head	qualifier (long describer)

News

determiner (pointing word)	numerative (quantity)	describer	classifier	head	qualifier (long describer)

Academic prose

determiner (pointing word)	numerative (quantity)	describer	classifier	head	qualifier (long describer)

CULTURE AND THE PACKAGING OF INFORMATION: CORPUS INSIGHTS AND INTERPRETIVE CAUTION

So far in this course, I hope you have been able to see the various insights that a corpus approach can bring. And as we have just seen, looking at the corpus results for common describers in noun phrases in English has confirmed that English is not something vast and uniform but is responsive to the situations in which it is produced. Aside from telling us about specific social situations, corpus investigations can enable us to zoom out from specific social situations and tell us something interesting about the culture in which we live. As you know, it is in noun phrases that information is packaged. If you can find out which are the most frequent noun phrases in a language, you can get a sense of what information can be regarded as significant in a culture. Take the noun *family*. This can function as a premodifier (classifier) of other nouns, as in: *family argument*, *family friend*, *family entertainment*. The Longman corpus tells us that the use of *family* in English as a premodifier is extremely **productive**. In this context, 'productive' refers to the wide-ranging use of a word in premodifying other nouns, i.e. the number of nouns it combines with. *School*, for example, combines with *book, girl, run*, etc. The corpus investigation confirms, it would seem, that the concept of the family is clearly important in US and UK cultures (i.e. the cultures from which the data for the corpus investigations were drawn).

Knowing that *family* is extremely productive in English might elicit the response: 'So what – I already knew that "family" is important in these cultures and so the corpus investigation just tells us what I could have worked out myself'. And I would concede that you have a point. But we might find out more interesting and illuminating things if we stop looking at English as a vast uniform thing and start splitting it up again. In splitting it up into the Longman registers, Biber et al. (1999) found that *family* as a premodifier showed up as extremely productive in news and much less so in conversation – it actually combines with more than 200 different head nouns in news. This comparison does not tell us that the concept of family is not important to people. But it might tell us that the concept of family is being constructed in news as being more significant than it really is for people. This may be because certain newspapers market themselves as 'family newspapers' when actually a large number of their readers are not so concerned about being targeted in this way. In news, nouns as premodifiers are much more productive than in any of the other Longman registers. Figure 1 comes from Biber et al. (1999). By examining it, you will see more clearly the point I am trying to make. ('Productivity' refers to the number of nouns that a premodifying noun occurs with, and not necessarily to its frequency.) Two levels of productivity are shown: nouns that are used in more than 50 different noun + noun sequences, and nouns that are used in more than 100 different noun + noun sequences.

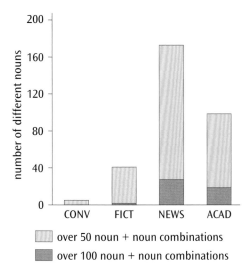

Figure 1 Productivity of premodifying nouns (Biber et al., 1999, p. 592)

Would you have known intuitively that news has by far the largest number of nouns that premodify head nouns? Would you have known that this is many times more than in conversation? News is both the reflector and shaper of cultures so to some extent highly productive premodifying nouns in news tell us something interesting about what newspapers regard as significant. We would have to be careful, though, what conclusions we might draw from the greater productivity of noun + noun sequences in news as compared with conversation. Just because a concept does not show up in a conversation corpus, it does not mean it is not important to people. Certain concepts may be important to people (e.g. religion) but they might not want to talk about them very much in company.

ACTIVITY 4 (allow about five minutes)

Interestingly, in news, there are only *four* classifier nouns that are both extremely productive (combining with more than 100 different head nouns) and extremely frequent (occurring as noun modifiers over 100 times per million words). Two such nouns which function as classifiers of head nouns are *world* and *home* (*world news*, *world cup*; *home office*, *home affairs*). See if you can guess what the other two might be for UK and US cultures. In other words, see if you can guess what the news industry in the US and the UK as a whole regards as significant.

COMMENT

One of these other very common premodifiers is *government*. This is commonly used as a classifier to premodify *action, agencies, approval, bonds, control, decision*. The other one is *police*, such as in *police force, police officer*. Perhaps this mirrors what is happening in the US/UK – large amounts of crime reports would naturally feature mention of the police. (In contrast, in some cultures where crime is not so high, *police* would presumably not be such a productive premodifier.) Or perhaps this indicates something about how the news shapes experience through giving more significance to *the police* through its productive use as a premodifier and its frequent use as a premodifier.

If you are not in the US or the UK, you might want to think about whether these productive premodifiers would be so productive in your print news media. If you do not think they would be, which ones do you think might be?

In the Longman news register, there are also around 150 additional premodifying nouns which are relatively productive (more than 50 combinations); most of these occur as noun modifiers fewer than 50 times per million words and they can be grouped as follows:

◆ business: *bank, company, consumer, insurance, management, price, trade (e.g. bank holiday, bank account)*

◆ the media: *film, media, newspaper, press, telephone, television (e.g. film premiere, film mogul)*

◆ other institutions: *prison, church, country, court, hospital, office (e.g. prison officer, prison governor)*

◆ sports: *football, soccer, sports, star, team (e.g. football player, football club).*

Overall, the extremely common use of nouns used as classifier premodifers in news results in a very dense, integrated packaging of information. This could be seen as fitting in with the need to save space in news reporting. This is certainly an explanation that Biber et al. (1999) give and for very short reports it seems to make sense. But the dense use of these forms places a heavy burden on readers. If I asked you to explain the meaning of *riot police* you would most likely unpack this noun phrase and turn it into a clause, i.e. *police who control riots*. I am sure you did not think *police who like to riot*! You unpacked the correct meaning without thinking about it. In this course, you have been introduced to noun + noun combinations such as *noun phrase, verb phrase, speech act, corpus analysis* – combinations that are part of the academic register. Would you have been able to unpack these before doing this course? Probably not.

So why can news reporting get away with so many noun + noun sequences, such as in the above examples, and academic English cannot without making demands on the reader?

You can see that the common semantic domains for news reporting are linked with current events, government, business, media, sports, police, world and home. Since these relate to fields for individual news reports with which readers would be expected to have some familiarity, journalists can expect readers to have well-developed knowledge and so be able to unpack noun + noun combinations without too much difficulty. As you saw in Unit 8, academic prose usually does not have such general fields, which means the non-specialist will experience more difficulty in unpacking noun + noun combinations in it.

ACTIVITY 5 (allow about 10 minutes)

Let us now focus on the Longman conversation register. You can see from Figure 1 that conversation represents the opposite extreme to news in this respect. It includes hardly any productive premodifying nouns. However, like the Longman news register, it has *four* premodifying nouns that are relatively productive (with more than 50 combinations). Do you think these four premodifiers will be the same as with those in the news register, i.e. *police*, *government*, *home* and *world*? Can you guess what they might be? In other words, what do you think might be commonly significant/important for speakers of English in the US and the UK?

COMMENT

It is interesting to compare the productivity of noun premodifiers in the Longman conversation register with those in the Longman news register because it might help us to see that what people talk about and regard as significant is not necessarily what the news industry regards as significant. In conversation, one of the four nouns that is notably productive as a noun premodifier in collocations is actually *Christmas*:

◆ Christmas + *cake, card, day, decorations, list, presents, tree*

Christmas is a major festive period in Britain and America and so the frequency of the premodifier *Christmas* should not be too surprising. The other three most common noun premodifiers in the Longman conversation corpus are *car*, *school* and *water*. Here are some common collocates for these nouns:

◆ car + *accident, door, insurance, keys, park, seat, wash*

◆ school + *book, children, clothes, fees, holidays, trips*

◆ water + *balloon, bottle, fight, leak, line, pressure, pump, rates*

Given that water is key to human survival and education so important in daily life, *water* and *school* are not surprising. As to *car*, its frequency as a premodifier tells us something (perhaps something depressing) about Western culture, consumption and lifestyle.

Comparing these results with those of the news corpus might tell us that many of us (perhaps also depressingly) are not so concerned with political issues – in conversation at least.

A CTIVITY 6 (allow about 10 minutes)

As you might have realised, we have to take care in how we interpret quantitative findings in the corpus. Can you see any problems with making the interpretations above of the four most productive noun premodifiers in conversation? Why might we have to consider *when* the corpus was compiled as a significant factor in how we interpret the findings? What else might we need to take into account in how we interpret the findings?

C OMMENT

We would have to know when the conversation corpus was compiled. If it was compiled in November/December, when Christmas is on people's minds, then it would not be surprising that *Christmas* showed up so productively as a noun premodifier. If the corpus had been compiled throughout the year, then we could make a stronger claim that Christmas is significant to people in the US and the UK. But we would have to be careful in saying that just because *Christmas* is a productive premodifier it is important to people. A sizeable portion of the corpus may show people bemoaning Christmas for its materialistic side. So *Christmas* might have occurred often in the corpus but actually it was being criticised. Lastly, the size of the corpus is also important. A small corpus of people chatting a few weeks before Christmas is not going to be very representative of the culture generally.

We have extended the discussion of premodification in noun phrases that was begun in Book 1 Unit 4. We have done this by dividing English into the different Longman registers and by looking at how the registers condition information-packaging. We can now move on to explore further differences in the way that information is packaged.

❸ PACKAGING INFORMATION: THE ROLE OF NOMINALISATION

We have extended the discussion initiated in Book 1 to see how classifiers and describers vary in their frequency and patterns of distribution across the four Longman registers of conversation, fiction, news, and academic writing. Having reviewed the role of the noun phrase in organising information, let us now return to the concept of nominalisation, which was first mentioned in Book 1 Unit 4.

A CTIVITY 7 (allow about 15 minutes)

Look at the two texts below, one of which you might remember from Unit 8, and answer these questions:

(1) What is the subject matter of each text?

(2) Which text sounds more spoken and which sounds more written?

(3) What grammatical differences between the two texts can you observe?

Text 3

The sex hormone estrogen is important for many physiologic processes. Prolonged stimulation of breast ductal epithelium by estrogen, however, can contribute to the development and progression of breast cancer, and treatments designed to block estrogen's effects are important options in the clinic. Tamoxifen and other similar drugs are effective in breast cancer prevention and treatment.

> (Osborne et al., 2000, pp. 3172–86; quoted in PubMed website, 4 September 2003)

Text 4

The sex hormone estrogen is really important for lots of physiologic processes. But if you use estrogen to stimulate the breast ductal epithelium for a long time, breast cancer can develop and progress. We have an important option in the clinic because we can treat patients by blocking the effects of estrogen. Tamoxifen and other similar drugs are effective because we can use them to both prevent and treat breast cancer.

C OMMENT

You should be able to see that the second text is more spoken than the first. You might also have been able to see that this is because it is less lexically dense. Text 3 has three sentences while Text 4 has four.

The main reason for this density is the number of nouns which describe a process in the first text, e.g. *stimulation, treatments, prevention, treatment, development, progression*. In Text 4, these are treated as processes rather than nouns.

> Prolonged stimulation of breast ductal epithelium by estrogen...

becomes

> ...if you use estrogen to stimulate the breast ductal epithelium for a long time, breast cancer can develop and progress.

You will see that more participants are created by expanding the ideas into clauses, for example *you* and *breast ductal epithelium*. As a result Text 4 is less compressed. It does not have the long and compressed subject participants that Text 3 has, for example *prolonged stimulation of breast ductal epithelium by estrogen*. Nouns such as *stimulation, treatments, prevention, treatment, development, progression* which are the results of compression of a process from a verb into a noun are known as nominalisations. Nominalisation refers to the tendency in English – especially technical English – to represent events, qualities of objects and qualities of events not as verbs, adjectives and adverbs but as nouns. The use of nominalisation increases dramatically in topics which are based on abstract concepts, properties and theories. In fact, without the ability to nominalise it would be impossible to conceive of many common concepts such as 'ownership', 'movement' or 'sexism', or to measure abstract things such as 'growth', 'birth rates', etc. Here are some examples of processes in their verb form and their nominalised form:

Verb form	Nominalised form
evaporate	evaporation
absorb	absorption
vibrate	vibration
to rain	the rain
to flow	the flow
deliver	delivery
arrive	arrival

Nominalisation is a significant move away from the everyday ways in which we talk about the world. There is a grammatical shift away from what we might expect in everyday language to more technical kinds of expression. This can be seen in the following transformation.

It got	quickly humid	and then	it came down cats and dogs.
	adjectival phrase		verb + adverbial phrase
clause 1		+	clause 2

This is now reworked as:

The rapid rise in humidity	was followed by	heavy precipitation.
noun phrase		noun phrase

You should be able to see that a clause complex, consisting of two clauses, has been transformed into one clause. This compression of information has been enabled by the nominalisations *humidity* and *precipitation*.

3.1 How is nominalisation used?

Nominalisation plays a key role in abstract/technical language for several reasons.

(a) It allows the formation of technical terms which stand for complex but commonly occurring – and commonly understood – phenomena.

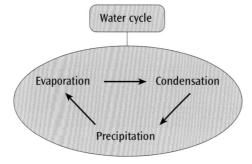

Figure 2

(b) It allows the development of abstract concepts and properties.

Many areas of knowledge deal not with 'real' tangible objects but with abstract concepts (for example, *evaporation, condensation* and *precipitation* from the verbs *evaporate, condense* and *precipitate* respectively, as in Figure 2).

(c) It allows us to make statements about cause-and-effect relationships between events. For example:

(d) It allows for the measurement, comparison and ordering of events.

Nominalisation allows us to represent events and qualities in language as 'things' rather than as 'processes' and adjectives. In English there are many more resources for measuring, comparing and ordering 'things' than there are for processes. When we use nominalisations, especially for abstract concepts and properties, we open up the possibility of precisely measuring and recording what was previously intangible. In technical fields this is particularly useful, since so much activity revolves around measuring, comparing and ordering.

To demonstrate the impact of nominalisation in this area, we look at two examples:

It rained.

It flooded.

If these events stay in verb form, we are limited to fairly qualitative, impressionistic means of measuring, ordering and comparing.
For example, we could say:

It rained heavily.

It rained for two hours.

It rained everywhere.

It rained like crazy.

In contrast, if we use the nominalised forms, *rain* or *rainfall*, there are many more resources available for describing the event. Moreover, the descriptions are more quantitative and precise in nature, and therefore compatible with scientific activity.

Measuring

25 mm of rain

heavy droplets of rain

large quantities of rain

Comparing

25% more rainfall

an increasing rate of rainfall

rainfall in the tropics

rainfall in desert regions

summer rainfall

winter rainfall

scattered rain

heavy rain

Ordering

the heaviest rainfall

the second heaviest rainfall

the most rain in the state

the most rain this century

(e) It allows the use of complex noun phrases to qualify and modify descriptions and explanations.

Form	Example
Verb form	It rained.
Nominalised form	The rainfall.
Nominalised form with describer	The increasing rainfall.
Nominalised form with qualifier	The increasing rainfall in the southern districts.

ACTIVITY 8   (allow about 15 minutes)

Identify the nominalisations in the following extract. Can you see examples where nominalisations are used:

◆ to create cause-and-effect relationships

◆ to create abstract properties or concepts

◆ to create technical terms

◆ to measure, order or compare phenomena

◆ as the base of a complex noun phrase?

See 'Answers to the activities' for feedback.

Ice movement

As much as 10 per cent of the Earth's present-day land area is covered by ice. We have evidence that, in the past, the area covered by ice was much greater.

In high mountain areas, large thicknesses of snow can collect. This is compressed by its own weight and hardened. The compression of the snow can cause it to form into large bodies of ice. The weight of the snow and ice causes the ice to move slowly down the valley. This moving body of ice is called a glacier.

The slow but powerful movement of this ice erodes sediments from the mountains and eventually carves out a large U-shaped valley, which is quite different from a river valley. The movement of the ice as it goes downhill also results in cracks, called crevasses, forming in the glacier.

The sediment that a glacier erodes from the mountains as it moves is deposited where the glacier melts. Unlike water and wind deposits, all the sediment is lumped together: large boulders with fine sand and even finer sediments. However, the melted glacier forms a river, which may carry some of the finer sediment further downstream. Any sediment formed by a glacier is called moraine. Deposits which form at the end of glaciers where they melt are called terminal moraines.

> (Adapted from Heffernan and Learmouth, 1988; quoted in *Exploring Literacy in School Science*, 1992, Metropolitan East Disadvantaged Schools Program, p. 134)

A CTIVITY 9   (allow about 30 minutes)

Now rewrite the first two paragraphs of the above text as though you might be speaking, using more processes than nominalisations. You will need to convert the nominalised forms into verbs, adjectives, etc.

See 'Answers to the activities' for feedback.

C OMMENT

By doing this exercise, you should see that putting things in the spoken mode makes experience more **congruent**, that is, in agreement with reality. Spoken language favours the clause, where processes take place, whereas written language favours the noun phrase, the location of the constitution of things. Written language tends to be more removed from – or less directly related to – the categories of our experience. In other words, written language tends to be more abstract. This in turn, if we are literate, affects our perceptions of what the world is like. The spoken form is 'nearer' to reality. It is usually more concrete, representing our experience in concrete ways, i.e. nouns are used to represent people and things, verbs are used to express doings and happenings, conjunctions are used to express logical connections.

Drift towards the noun

In order to move from the concrete towards the less concrete and more abstract, English makes use of the noun. The drift towards the noun (via a process of nominalisation) is illustrated in the examples which follow.

From verb to noun:

> they *announced* it, then people *applauded*
>> <u>after</u> they had *announced* it, people *applauded*
>>> <u>after</u> the *announcement*, people *applauded*
>>>> applause followed the announcement

From conjunction to noun:

> *a* happened, <u>so</u> *x* happened
>> *x* happened <u>because</u> *a* happened
>>> *x* happened <u>because of</u> happening *a*
>>>> happening *a* <u>caused</u> happening *x*
>>>>> happening *a* was <u>the cause of</u> happening *x*

This drift towards the noun and thus towards abstraction is part of what makes some English registers, such as academic English, less easy to process. This drift is explored in the reading in the next activity.

A CTIVITY 10 (allow about three hours)

Read Chapter 5, 'Some Grammatical Problems in Scientific English' by M. A. K. Halliday in the course reader, *Applying English Grammar*.

In this reading, you will see that Halliday discusses a number of different aspects of scientific English which can cause difficulties. Read the article to find out what these are. One difficulty which Halliday highlights, and which relates to the drift towards abstraction in scientific English, he refers to as **grammatical metaphor**. Make notes on what this is and why grammatical metaphor in English can cause problems for students of science. In the article, Halliday uses terminology such as **thing** for a head noun and **deictic** for a determiner.

COMMENT

You should have found that much of the reading confirmed what you did in Activity 9. Since conversation is more clause-oriented, it reflects experience more than written registers do. When we utter *Susan kicked the ball excellently in the football game* as a report of what we experienced, we can say that the clause order of participant–process–circumstance construes the event in the order in which we caught the experience. That is, we say that the experiential meaning in the clause is congruent with the actual experience. Nominalisation of clauses – *Susan's excellent ball-kicking* – reduces congruency because we no longer have the participant–process–circumstance order. As you will have read, Halliday treats the participant–process–circumstance order as primary because as children we first learn to speak following this pattern. (Certainly if we take the spoken mode as being more congruent with experience, the fact that clauses are more common in speech than in writing is supported by corpus evidence: see your reference grammar.) It is only later – when we can read and write with facility – that we are able to turn clauses into noun phrases. You will have read that Halliday treats this reworking of clauses into phrases as metaphor: grammatical metaphor, he calls it. Instead of being a substitution of one word for another as in lexical metaphor (for example, *You're talking rubbish* instead of *You're talking nonsense*) grammatical metaphor involves a substitution of one grammatical structure by another. You will have seen that nominalisation is actually only one form of grammatical metaphor and that Halliday refers to other types. As consolidation, let us look at an example of grammatical metaphor which is not nominalisation. Here is a sentence in the spoken mode which has been transformed into the written mode:

Spoken mode

Because the electrons in the two atoms are absolutely indistinguishable, they attract each other 'extra' strongly.

Written mode equivalent (academic register)

The absolute indistinguishability of the electrons in the two atoms gives rise to an 'extra' attractive force between them.

To see where the grammatical metaphor has taken place, let us analyse functionally:

(a)

Because	the electrons in the two atoms	are	absolutely indistinguishable
relator	participant	process	participant
they	attract	each other	strongly.
participant	process	participant	circumstance

(A **relator** expresses relations between clauses.)

(b)

The absolute indistinguishability of the electrons in the two atoms	gives rise to	a strong attractive force	between them.
participant	process	participant	circumstance

From the perspective of function, *because* as a relator is congruent in the spoken mode. The spoken mode is clausal and so will need relators to link clauses together. Hence, relators are congruent with reality.

In the written mode, the relator has been metaphorised into a process. This is an example of grammatical metaphor but it is not a nominalisation. If we wanted to give it a name as a subcategory of grammatical metaphor we might call it 'processisation'. At the level of grammatical class, a conjunction has become a verb. There has also been a shift down the rank scale – the clause complex in (a) has become a single clause in (b). The initial clause in (a) also shifts down the rank scale by becoming a noun phrase (see Book 1 Units 3 and 6 on rank scale).

You should also be able to see another type of grammatical metaphor, the type I have mainly focused on in this section: nominalisation. The adjective *indistinguishable* has become a noun, *indistinguishability*. The quality *indistinguishable* has now been incorporated into a complex noun phrase where *indistinguishability* is a head noun and the head in the spoken mode, *the electrons*, has been transformed into a postmodifier in the written mode. You should also be able to see that metaphorising the quality, *indistinguishable*, into a head, *indistinguishability*, enables not only postmodification with an 'of-phrase' but also the postmodification of the first participant in the spoken version, *in the two atoms*, to be transferred into postmodification of *the electrons*, something which is also a postmodifier. Experiential meaning is particularly compacted since what follows *indistinguishability* is actually a postmodifier complex. The creation of abstraction is also reflected by the extra determiner *the*. Indeed, there is clearly a relationship between the frequency of articles and of nouns in a particular register. More 'compact' registers like the academic register will naturally have more nouns and so these nouns are more likely to be modified by articles. This is less the case with the spoken mode, where there is more use of clauses. The diagram below shows these relative frequencies.

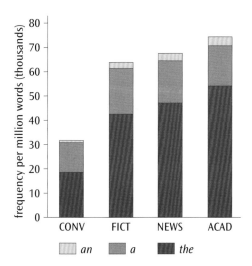

Figure 3 Distribution of definite and indefinite articles across registers (Biber et al., 1999, p. 267)

When you do the CD-ROM activities, you will come across more examples of grammatical metaphor.

The first three sections of this unit have been concerned with packaging information. The last section will be concerned with organising and staging information.

◆4 STAGING INFORMATION IN A CLAUSE

Let us start this section by examining two texts in order to see how the speakers/writers differ in terms of how they organise their ideas and information.

◆ACTIVITY 11 (allow about 30 minutes)

Read the two texts overleaf and answer the following questions.

1   What is the general field of the two texts?

   (a)   academia

   (b)   education

   (c)   school history

2   What kind of relationship is established between writer and reader in the texts?

   (a)   personal and close

   (b)   impersonal and distant

   (c)   one of solidarity

3   What do you think the overall communicative purpose of the two texts is?

   (a)   to argue that, despite being a female and a convict, a person can still be successful

   (b)   to record the main events in Mary Reibey's life

   (c)   to explain why Mary Reibey became famous

4   Do you notice anything about the way information is organised in the two texts?

Text 5

Mary Reibey

Mary Reibey nee Haydock was born in England in 1772. She was transported as a convict to Australia where she became a successful business woman.

In 1785, at the age of thirteen, Mary was convicted for stealing the favourite horse of the local squire. She was sentenced, as a result, to seven years transportation to New South Wales. Soon after, she was employed as a nursemaid in the household of Major Francis Grose.

Nine years later, in 1794, Mary married Thomas Reibey, a young officer of the British East India Company. They set up a home in the Rocks area where she ran a bakery business while her husband operated a fleet of three small ships to the Hawkesbury for grain and the Hunter River for coal and timber. During this time she also managed to raise seven children.

In 1809 Thomas Reibey suffered severe sunstroke in India and died two years later. Mary therefore took over the family businesses, many of which were located in the centre of Sydney.

1812 was the year that Mary opened a new warehouse and expanded her maritime business by buying a ship called the John Palmer. In 1817 she bought another ship.

Three years later she returned to England with her daughters to visit family and friends and at the same time took care of her business interests.

In 1828 she returned to Sydney to continue making investments in city properties. She became involved in charity work, town planning and education.

On the 30th of May, 1855 Mary died in Newtown, NSW, aged seventy-eight.

Mary Reibey, despite her convict background, became one of the few successful female convicts. She was an extremely competent business woman. As well, she was a selfless person. She received great respect from the community due to her charity work. Her life was indeed fortunate.

(Adapted from 'Australian Identity', *Write it Right*, 1996, p. 63)

Text 6

Mary Reibey

Mary Reibey nee Haydock was born in England in 1772. She was transported as a convict to Australia where she became a successful business woman.

Mary was convicted for stealing the favourite horse of the local squire in 1785, at the age of thirteen. She was sentenced, as a result, to seven years transportation to New South Wales. She was employed as a nursemaid in the household of Major Francis Grose soon after she arrived.

Mary married Thomas Reibey, a young officer of the British East India Company, nine years later, in 1794. They set up a home in the Rocks area where she ran a bakery business while her husband operated a fleet of three small ships to the Hawkesbury for grain and the Hunter River for coal and timber. She also managed to raise seven children during this time.

Thomas Reibey suffered severe sunstroke in India in 1809 and died two years later. Mary therefore took over the family businesses, many of which were located in the centre of Sydney.

Mary opened a new warehouse and expanded her maritime business by buying a ship called the John Palmer in 1812. She bought another ship in 1817.

She returned to England with her daughters to visit family and friends three years later and at the same time took care of her business interests.

She returned to Sydney to continue making investments in city properties in 1828. She became involved in charity work, town planning and education.

Mary died in Newtown, NSW, aged seventy-eight, on the 30th of May, 1855.

Mary Reibey, despite her convict background, became one of the few successful female convicts. She was an extremely competent business woman. As well, she was a selfless person. She received great respect from the community due to her charity work. Her life was indeed fortunate.

(Adapted from 'Australian Identity', *Write it Right*, 1996, p. 63)

COMMENT

You will probably have deduced that both texts were produced by secondary school students for assessment by their teacher. You will also probably have decided that, although they could be regarded as academic prose, the fact that they were produced for educational purposes, and specifically within the field of history, means that a more precise description of their field is school history. In fact we could be even more precise in our description and say the field is the life of Mary Reibey within the more general field of school history.

In answer to Question 2, it is likely that you chose (b) impersonal and distant. In keeping with the conventions of school writing for assessment purposes, the relationship between student and teacher is relatively formal rather than chatty and familiar.

With regard to the communicative purpose of the texts, we can say that the primary purpose of the writer is to record the main events in Mary Reibey's life. That is, even though through the retelling of these events we find out some of the reasons for Mary Reibey's fame, the primary point of departure is not: *There are three main reasons why Mary Reibey is a well-known name in Australian History*, etc. Instead we are taken through a chronological record of events in Reibey's life.

This leads us to the final question regarding the way information is organised in the two texts. Clearly both texts are written and organised into a series of paragraphs, each of which covers a key event in Reibey's life. What is strikingly different about their organisation, however, is the departure point for each of these paragraphs. Whereas circumstances of time (see Book 1 Unit 3) are in first position in many of the opening sentences of each of Text 5's paragraphs, they are in final position in Text 6. Thus:

Text 5

Nine years later, in 1784, Mary married Thomas Reibey, a young officer of the British East India Company

compared with:

Text 6

Mary married Thomas Reibey, a young officer of the British East India Company, nine years later, in 1784.

You may remember from Book 1 Unit 3 that in English grammar (unlike some languages) many of the elements in a clause can be reordered to have different communicative effects. Thus you saw in that unit how clauses which have essentially the same experiential content can be organised in quite different ways. You started with the sentence:

We had a fantastic rabbit dish at the restaurant on our way back to our villa from the market one day.

And saw possible variations, for example:

> At the restaurant, we had a fantastic rabbit dish on our way back to our villa from the market one day.

> On our way back to our villa from the market one day, we had a fantastic rabbit dish at the restaurant.

> One day, we had a fantastic rabbit dish at the restaurant on our way back to our villa from the market.

You can see how what is underlined varies in each of these examples. These sentences demonstrate how what comes first at clause level can vary considerably, so the choices exercised by speakers and writers in this regard are functional and meaningful. That is, we start a message from a different point depending on what information is relevant and meaningful to our communicative purpose and our audience.

To go back to the Mary Reibey texts, in Text 5 the dates and the intervals of time are in first place in many of the opening paragraph clauses in order to provide the reader with time as a 'backbone' of meaning and relevance all the way through the text. This seems an appropriate organising principle for a text whose purpose is to record events in a chronological order. In Text 6, on the other hand, the participant, *Mary Reibey*, is reiterated in first position and perhaps, as a result, the reader has less of a sense of moving through time.

The technical term for the first element or departure point in a clause is **theme**. The use of the term 'theme' in functional grammar needs to be distinguished from its more general (often literary) use, which refers to the most important or general messages in a work of art, film, public talk, etc. In functional grammar, in contrast, 'theme' is formally defined as stretching as far as and including the first experiential element in a clause – that is a participant, process or circumstance. What follows it in a clause is called the **rheme**. The rheme is the part of the clause which develops the theme, for example:

> Nine years later, in 1784, Mary married Thomas Reibey, a young officer of the British East India Company.

Theme = *Nine years, later in 1784*

This is a circumstance and hence an experiential element – and therefore satisfies the definition of theme above.

Rheme = *Mary married Thomas Reibey, a young officer of the British East India Company*

This develops the theme, and is therefore the rheme because it tells us what happened nine years later, in 1784.

Theme was first mentioned in Unit 7 of Book 1. It will be revisited in Unit 14 of Book 3, and reviewed in Unit 17 of Book 4.

A CTIVITY 12 (allow about 20 minutes)

Using the definition of 'theme' on the previous page, work your way through Text 5 underlining all the themes in each of the sentences. (For the moment do not worry if the sentence has more than one clause.)

See 'Answers to the activities' for feedback.

COMMENT

You will have noticed from your analysis in Activity 11 that, aside from circumstances of time, the other main starting point for Text 5 is the participant, *Mary Reibey*. Given that Reibey is the main focus of the text this is not surprising. The part of the theme which consists of circumstance(s), process or participant is referred to as the topical or **experiential theme** – processes, participants and circumstances are concerned with experiential meaning, as you will remember from Unit 8.

A CTIVITY 13 (allow about 20 minutes)

Now you are going to practise finding themes in one of the texts that you have already seen in Unit 8. Underline the themes in each of the clauses (which we have already identified for you with the symbol ‖). Remember that you need to underline all the words *up to and including* the first experiential element (either a participant, process or circumstance). We have already completed a few of these as examples. You will notice that the phrase *ellipsed theme* occurs occasionally in brackets. This is because where there is ellipsis of the subject (see Book 1 Unit 1) we say there is no experiential theme. Likewise there is no theme where there is a non-finite verb in initial position in the clause.

Researchers follow slightly different practices on this point. In Unit 17 of Book 4, we shall include ellipsed experiential themes in our analysis. You will also find that the Activities CD-ROM includes ellipsed themes.

Text 7

<u>The sex hormone estrogen</u> is important for many physiologic processes. ‖ <u>Prolonged stimulation of breast ductal epithelium by estrogen</u>, however, can contribute to the development and progression of breast cancer, ‖ <u>and treatments designed to block estrogen's effects</u> are important options in the clinic.‖ Tamoxifen and other similar drugs are effective in breast cancer prevention and treatment ‖ by inhibiting the proliferative effects of estrogen that are mediated through the estrogen receptor (ER). ‖ However, these drugs also have many estrogenic effects ‖ depending on the tissue and gene, ‖ and they are more appropriately called selective

estrogen receptor modulators (SERMs). ‖ SERMs bind ER, ‖ alter receptor conformation, (*ellipsed theme*) ‖ and (*ellipsed theme*) facilitate binding of coregulatory proteins that activate or repress transcriptional activation of estrogen target genes. ‖ Theoretically, SERMs could be synthesized that would exhibit nearly complete agonist activity on the one hand or pure antiestrogenic activity on the other. ‖ Depending on their functional activities, ‖ SERMs could then be developed for a variety of clinical uses, ‖ including prevention and treatment of osteoporosis, treatment and prevention of estrogen-regulated malignancies, and even for hormone replacement therapy. ‖ Tamoxifen is effective in patients with ER-positive metastatic breast cancer and in the adjuvant setting. ‖ The promising role for tamoxifen in ductal carcinoma-in-situ or for breast cancer prevention is evolving, ‖ and its use can be considered in certain patient groups. ‖ Other SERMs are in development, with the goal of reducing toxicity and/or improving efficacy.

(Osborne et al., 2000, pp. 3172–86; quoted in PubMed website, 4 September 2003)

See 'Answers to the activities' for feedback.

COMMENT

In carrying out Activity 13 you will probably have noticed that the theme can be quite lengthy in academic writing, consisting of dense nominalised noun phrases. For example:

> ‖ and <u>treatments designed to block estrogen's effects</u> are important options in the clinic

We will contrast theme in academic writing with theme in other registers a little later and you will see that the length and density of the theme typically correlates with its register and, specifically, with its mode, i.e. how spontaneous and interactive a text is.

In Text 7 you will have noticed that many of the themes consist only of experiential elements in the form of participants. However, you may also have noticed that, in some clauses, the theme includes elements which are not only experiential elements. Remember the definition of theme: anything up to and including the first experiential element in a clause. Thus a theme could include not only experiential elements but textual and interpersonal elements too. Let us start with textual elements in a theme. Thinking back to the contextual framework set up in Unit 8, what sort of function might a textual element in a theme have? (Go back to the section on mode in Unit 8 if you need to remind yourself of the main dimensions of mode.) A textual element in a theme will serve to link one clause with another. Take, for example, the following from the text you just analysed:

and	treatments designed to block estrogen's effects	are important options in the clinic
textual theme (coordinator)	experiential theme	
	theme	rheme

The **textual theme** *and* is a coordinator which serves to link what follows it with the previous clause. But this textual element is not the whole theme because, as you will remember from the definition of theme, we also need an experiential element. Above we have the participant *treatments designed to block estrogen's effects*. It should be clear, then, that theme can be subdivided into different elements, here a textual and an experiential element. These different elements are still referred to as experiential themes and textual themes even though they are really only elements in the actual theme.

Now you know that themes can be subdivided into experiential themes and textual themes. There is also a third subdivision – interpersonal themes. What do you think is the function of the **interpersonal theme** in the (larger) theme? Look at the following examples. How is the interpersonal theme functioning? Again, think back to the contextual framework in Unit 8. What are the main dimensions of tenor and the main language features that serve to build interpersonal meaning?

Perhaps	you	need some turnips.
interpersonal theme	experiential theme	
	theme	rheme

Darling	you	need some turnips.
interpersonal theme	experiential theme	
	theme	rheme

Having reminded yourself of the interpersonal metafunction, you should be able to see that the interpersonal theme *perhaps* in the first example above adds information about the speaker's stance. He/she is not sure whether the listener needs some turnips. It could also be that the speaker is being polite and is forming the statement in an indirect way. In the second sentence, the interpersonal theme *darling* is a term of address and so tells us something about the relationship between speaker and listener or about how the speaker wishes to construct the relationship, and so on. These interpersonal themes are significant since they are in the departure point for the message and thus will affect how the rheme is understood by the listener.

Interpersonal themes also play a role in the interrogative mood, both **wh-interrogatives** (interrogatives with wh-question words like *what, why,* *where, when* and *how*) and **polar interrogatives** (interrogatives that require a yes or no answer). Since wh-words are also circumstances and thus an experiential element, they form the whole of the theme, as in:

Where	did you buy some turnips?
interpersonal and experiential theme (circumstance)	
theme	rheme

Finites in interrogatives such as *does, did, have, has*, etc., are not experiential elements and cannot comprise the whole theme. The whole theme in polar interrogatives comprises the finite and the subject:

Did	you	buy some turnips?
interpersonal theme (finite)	experiential theme (subject)	
theme		rheme

A CTIVITY 14 (allow about 20 minutes)

You have looked at themes in two academic texts so far. Let us now continue exploring themes by comparing across three of the Longman registers. I include the academic text you looked at in the last activity. But I also include a conversational text and a news text – you will recognise all three texts from Unit 8. I want you to go through all the texts looking for themes: identify the experiential, interpersonal and textual themes that make up each theme proper. In each of the clauses (which I have already identified for you with the symbol ‖) indicate the themes by underlining them. I have already completed a few of these as examples. Using different colours to underline the themes will make things clearer for you.

Note: in minor clauses (i.e. where there is no verb) there is no theme. In dependent finite clauses, a subordinator usually functions as a textual theme, followed by an experiential theme, e.g. *They knew* ‖ *that* (textual) *in spring the snow would melt*. Non-finite clauses sometimes contain textual and experiential themes, e.g. *With* (textual) *all the doors being locked* ‖ *we had no way in*. However, usually they consist only of a rheme, e.g. *To avoid delay* ‖ *have your money ready*.

Then look at the overall pattern of theme choices in each text. Can you think why they are so different across the three texts from the three different Longman registers?

Key to transcription: '+' indicates that the word has been cut short – the complete word has not been fully articulated or could not be transcribed.

Text 8

SPEAKER 1 <u>How</u> do you find the local GP? ‖

SPEAKER 2 <u>Oh he</u>'s all right. ‖

SPEAKER 1 <u>Which</u> ... which surgery are you at? ‖

SPEAKER 2 Er [Name-of-Road] Street. (*ellipsed theme*)

SPEAKER 1 [Name-of-Road] Street. (*ellipsed theme*)

SPEAKER 2 Mm. Dr [Name-of-Doctor], he's very good ‖ but as I say ‖ we don't run to a doctor for nothing, ‖ y' know ‖ what I mean. ‖ But we've had <coughs> had us jabs for flu. ‖ I got a lump on the back of my neck ‖ so we h+ ‖ I had to have what was it called?

SPEAKER 3 Antibiotics (*ellipsed theme*)

SPEAKER 2 Antibiotics (*ellipsed theme*) and it must have helped it to burst or summat ‖ and now of course it's pretty much gone. ‖ And that was it with me.

[...]

SPEAKER 2 I had skin cancer. ‖ I'd been digging in the garden ‖ and and I don't know ‖ whether I scratched myself with a <pause> ‖ 'cos I was doing my <pause> ‖ I don't ‖ whether a s+ a thorn caught me on the nose ‖ and then I'd been digging

SPEAKER 1 Mm.

SPEAKER 2 Cats and all sorts had been digging about, ‖ I hate cats, ‖ and it wouldn't heal up ‖ and it was going on ‖ and I was getting cream cream on my nose – ‖ it never ha+ healed up ‖ you see. ‖ So I went to the doctor's ‖ and they looked at it down the infirmary. ‖ Then they had to have those all these specialists round ‖ you you know ‖ and I thought, ‖ Why the heck am I seeing other people. ‖ Anyway they had to have ten

(Collins Cobuild Bank of English: subcorpus = brspok/UK)

Text 9

TURNIPS 'CURE SARS'

Demand for veg rockets in killer bug scare

<u>SALES of turnips</u> are rocketing in China ‖ <u>because the veg</u> is said ‖ to cure SARS. ‖

<u>They</u> are used in herbal remedies sold to treat severe acute respiratory syndrome. ‖

Wholesale prices of turnips in China's capital Beijing have shot up
THIRTY PER CENT in a week amid fears over the deadly flu-like
virus. ‖ Carrots, garlic and ginger are also included in the potions ‖
and shops have been selling out. ‖

The global death toll from SARS rose to 153 yesterday. ‖ Nine were
reported in Hong Kong -the most in one day there so far. ‖ They
included a woman aged 34, who died while giving birth. ‖

The condition of the baby was not known. ‖

China has been hit hardest by SARS, with 64 deaths. ‖

One newspaper in the country has recommended dead silkworms
in one remedy. ‖

There is still no recognised cure for SARS, ‖ which has infected
more than 3,300 people in at least 20 countries ‖ since it emerged in
southern China last November. ‖

However, a German company said yesterday ‖ it had developed a
high-speed test for the virus. ‖

Artus, based in Hamburg, said ‖ it could detect SARS in two hours. ‖

Current checks can take up to ten days. ‖

Artus said ‖ it would distribute the test free to laboratories
worldwide. ‖

Manager Thomas Laue said: ‖ 'It will be our share in controlling
this plague.' ‖

Seven people in Britain have been treated so far for SARS symptoms. ‖

Four have recovered ‖ and been discharged from hospital. (*ellipsed
topical theme*)

(Russell, *The Sun*, 16 April 2003)

Text 10

The sex hormone estrogen is important for many physiologic
processes. ‖ Prolonged stimulation of breast ductal epithelium by
estrogen, however, can contribute to the development and
progression of breast cancer, ‖ and treatments designed to block
estrogen's effects are important options in the clinic. ‖ Tamoxifen and
other similar drugs are effective in breast cancer prevention and
treatment ‖ by inhibiting the proliferative effects of estrogen that are
mediated through the estrogen receptor (ER). ‖ However, these drugs
also have many estrogenic effects ‖ depending on the tissue and gene, ‖
and they are more appropriately called selective estrogen receptor
modulators (SERMs). ‖ SERMs bind ER, ‖ alter receptor conformation,
‖ (*ellipsed theme*) ‖ and (*ellipsed theme*) facilitate binding of coregulatory
proteins that activate or repress transcriptional activation of estrogen
target genes. ‖ Theoretically, SERMs could be synthesized that

would exhibit nearly complete agonist activity on the one hand or pure antiestrogenic activity on the other. ‖ Depending on their functional activities, ‖ SERMs could then be developed for a variety of clinical uses, ‖ including prevention and treatment of osteoporosis, treatment and prevention of estrogen-regulated malignancies, and even for hormone replacement therapy. ‖ Tamoxifen is effective in patients with ER-positive metastatic breast cancer and in the adjuvant setting. ‖ The promising role for tamoxifen in ductal carcinoma-in-situ or for breast cancer prevention is evolving, ‖ and its use can be considered in certain patient groups. ‖ Other SERMs are in development, with the goal of reducing toxicity and/or improving efficacy.

(Osborne et al., 2000, pp. 3172–86; quoted in PubMed website, 4 September 2003)

COMMENT

From your completed analysis (also see 'Answers to the activities' section) you will have found that in the conversational text many of the themes are participants in the form of pronouns (e.g. *I, you*). In addition there are interpersonal themes in the form of interrogative words (*how, why*). The themes thus reflect the to-ing and fro-ing of interactive and spontaneous conversation.

In the news text, in contrast, the experiential themes are often non-human participants expressed in the form of noun phrases (e.g. *wholesale prices of turnips, the global death toll from SARS, the condition of the baby*). In news, therefore, the starting point for the clause is often information that is newsworthy (e.g. *the global death toll*). Where there are human participants, the social standing of the participant is often **thematised**, i.e. is placed in initial position (*Manager Thomas Laue...; a German company...*). This gives credibility to the reported statements that follow.

The textual themes in the news text are linking words which express cause (*because*) and contrast (*however*) whereas in the conversation text the main linking word is *and*. News, in other words, attempts to make causal connections between events whereas in unplanned conversation the relationship between events is often one of addition, with participants stringing clauses together moment by moment.

When we compare theme choices in the academic text (Text 10) with those in the news report and the conversation, the most striking difference is the increases in dense, compact noun phrases and in the extent of nominalisation. Clearly it is important for the readers of this text to be given precise technical terms (e.g. *the sex hormone estrogen*). In addition the focus, rather than being on the person writing the article or on those responsible for developing the medical treatments, is on the drugs themselves as well as the kinds of treatment made possible.

4.1 Mood and theme: the concept of marked and unmarked theme

Above we drew attention to one form of mood found in the themes of Text 8 in particular: the interrogative. For the sake of clarity and comprehensiveness, we want to contrast our analysis of theme for interrogatives with other moods and introduce one final concept in relation to theme – **marked theme**. The default patterns of theme are the ones which match the declarative, interrogative and imperative patterns, but speakers and writers can vary these patterns to orient a clause in a particular way. First, let us revise each of these mood structures, which we first came across in Book 1 Unit 3, and see what typically comes first.

Declarative (theme = subject)

> They went to the beach.

Interrogative: wh (theme = wh-word)

> Where did they go?

Interrogative: polar (theme = finite + subject)

> Did they go to the beach?

Imperative (theme = process)

> Go to the beach!

Typically in a declarative clause the subject and the theme are the same, but often speakers/writers vary this expected or **unmarked** starting point to achieve a variety of effects. For example, as we saw in the Mary Reibey texts, circumstances rather than participants may be thematised:

> (a) Nine years later, in 1784, Mary married Thomas Reibey, a young officer of the British East India Company.

as opposed to

> (b) Mary married Thomas Reibey, a young officer of the British East India Company, nine years later, in 1784.

Where a theme and subject in a declarative clause are not the same, as in (a), we call the theme marked. So, in a clause like *Thomas Reibey Mary married*, the theme is the complement, not the subject of the clause, making it marked. As a term, marked means atypical or unusual (see Unit 7).

In both spoken and written texts there may be other types of theme variation. In the following sentences, for example, why do you think the speaker/writer used the system of voice to thematise *Europeans* in one sentence and *Australia* in the other?

ACTIVE: <u>Europeans</u> colonised Australia in 1788.

PASSIVE: <u>Australia</u> was colonised in 1788.

In Unit 11 we shall think further about why it may sometimes be effective to thematise the actor (the *Europeans* in the example above) rather than the goal (*Australia* in the example above). Over the next couple of weeks keep your eyes open to see which actors get thematised in news reports.

ACTIVITIES CD-ROM (allow about four hours)

Now work through the activities for this unit on the Activities CD-ROM.

Conclusion

In this unit you have looked at how information is packaged and staged across the four Longman registers of fiction, academic writing, conversation and news. As a result of examining texts from these registers and seeing some poor examples, you should be in a better position to be able to package and stage meaning effectively in your own writing.

Learning outcomes

After completing Unit 9, you should have developed your knowledge and understanding of:

◆ the concept of mode

◆ the role of nominalisation in packaging information

◆ the concept of theme in relation to how information is staged in a clause.

You should have developed your ability to:

◆ *describe* grammatical features of a text in relation to the concept of mode

◆ *interpret* texts and their grammatical features with regard to mode.

Finally, let us see what territory has been mapped up to this point:

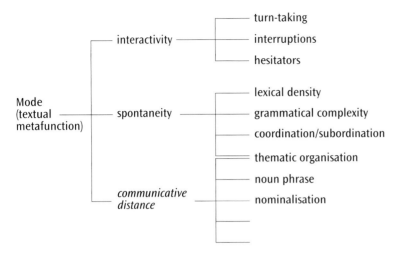

Figure 4 Map of mode (italics indicate an aspect of mode to be introduced later in the course)

Key terms introduced and revisited	
classifier	polar interrogative
collocation	productive
congruent	qualifier
deictic	rank scale
describer	relator
determiner	rheme
experiential theme [topical theme]	textual theme
grammatical metaphor	thematise
head	theme
interpersonal theme	thing
marked theme	unmarked theme
nominalisation	wh-interrogative
numerative	

Near equivalents are given in [ ].

Answers to the activities

ACTIVITY 1

Determiner (pointing words)	Numerative (quantity)	Describer	Classifier	Head	Qualifier (long describer)
the		bland	May	sunshine	
a		luxurious		purple	
			regular	lines	of emerald green
	rising (describer) heaps of	humpy yellow		rock	
a				band	of lighter green, icy and pure, less radiant
the		bright		sunshine	
the		gentle		water	
a			surface	skin	of colour
the		cloudless		sky	
the		indigo		horizon	

ACTIVITY 2

Describer	Classifier	Head	Qualifier
hot, brooding		May	
bright		mangoes	
still, dustgreen		trees	
red		bananas	
dissolute		bluebottles	
fruity		air	
clear		windowpanes	
sullen		expectation	

Original text

May in Ayemenem is a hot, brooding month. The days are long and humid. The river shrinks and black crows gorge on bright mangoes in still, dust green trees. Red bananas ripen. Jackfruits burst. Dissolute bluebottles hum vacuously in the fruity air. Then they stun themselves against clear windowpanes and die, fatly baffled in the sun.

The nights are clear but suffused with sloth and sullen expectation.

(Roy, 1997, p. 1)

ACTIVITY 8

Nominalisations are underlined:

Ice movement

As much as 10 per cent of the Earth's present day land area is covered by ice. We have evidence that, in the past, the area covered by ice was much greater.

In high mountain areas, large thicknesses of snow can collect. This is compressed by its own weight and hardened. The compression of the snow can cause it to form into large bodies of ice. The weight of the snow and ice causes the ice to move slowly down the valley. This moving body of ice is called a glacier.

The slow but powerful movement of this ice erodes sediments from the mountains and eventually carves out a large U-shaped valley, which is quite different from a river valley. The movement of the ice as it goes downhill also results in cracks, called crevasses, forming in the glacier.

The sediment that a glacier erodes from the mountains as it moves is deposited where the glacier melts. Unlike water and wind deposits, all the sediment is lumped together; large boulders with fine sand and even finer sediments. However, the melted glacier forms a river, which may carry some of the finer sediment further downstream. Any sediment formed by a glacier is called moraine. Deposits which form at the end of glaciers where they melt are called terminal moraines.

(Adapted from Heffernan and Learmouth, 1988; quoted in *Exploring Literacy in School Science*, 1992, Metropolitan East Disadvantaged Schools Program, p.134)

The compression of the snow can cause it to form into large bodies of ice creates a cause-and-effect relationship.

Unlike water and wind deposits, all the sediment is lumped together; large boulders with fine sand and even finer sediments creates an abstract property/concept.

Deposits which form at the end of glaciers where they melt are called terminal moraines creates a technical term.

The slow but powerful <u>movement</u> of this ice erodes sediments from the mountains and eventually carves out a large U-shaped valley, which is quite different from a river valley measures/orders/compares phenomena.

The nominalised *movement* in *The slow but powerful <u>movement</u> of this ice* is the base of a complex noun phrase.

ACTIVITY 9

Ice movement

As much as 10 per cent of the Earth's present-day land area is covered by ice. We have evidence that, in the past, the area covered by ice was much greater.

In high mountain areas, thick snow can collect in large amounts. Being so big and heavy, the snow becomes compressed and hardens. The weight of the snow compresses it to such an extent that it forms into large bodies of ice. The snow weighs so much that it moves the ice slowly down the valley. This moving body of ice is called a glacier.

As the ice moves slowly but powerfully down the valley it erodes sediments from the mountains and eventually carves out a large U-shaped valley, which is quite different from a river valley. As the ice moves downhill it also cracks open part of the glacier producing what are called crevasses.

(Adapted from Heffernan and Learmouth, 1988; quoted in *Exploring Literacy in School Science*, 1992, Metropolitan East Disadvantaged Schools Program, p.134)

ACTIVITY 12

The themes are underlined below.

Mary Reibey

<u>Mary Reibey nee Haydock</u> was born in England in 1772. <u>She</u> was transported as a convict to Australia where she became a successful business woman.

<u>In 1785</u>, at the age of thirteen, Mary was convicted for stealing the favourite horse of the local squire. <u>She</u> was sentenced, as a result, to seven years transportation to New South Wales. <u>Soon after,</u> she was employed as a nursemaid in the household of Major Francis Grose.

<u>Nine years later, in 1784</u>, Mary married Thomas Reibey, a young officer of the British East India Company. <u>They</u> set up a home in the Rocks area where she ran a bakery business while her husband operated a fleet of three small ships to the Hawkesbury for grain and

the Hunter River for coal and timber. <u>During this time</u> she also managed to raise seven children.

<u>In 1809</u> Thomas Reibey suffered severe sunstroke in India and died two years later. <u>Mary</u> therefore took over the family businesses, many of which were located in the centre of Sydney.

<u>1812</u> was the year that Mary opened a new warehouse and expanded her maritime business by buying a ship called the John Palmer. <u>In 1817</u> she bought another ship.

<u>Three years later</u> she returned to England with her daughters to visit family and friends and at the same time took care of her business interests.

<u>In 1828</u> she returned to Sydney to continue making investments in city properties. <u>She</u> became involved in charity work, town planning and education.

<u>On the 30th of May, 1855</u> Mary died in Newtown, NSW, aged seventy-eight.

<u>Mary Reibey</u>, despite her convict background, became one of the few successful female convicts. <u>She</u> was an extremely competent business woman. <u>As well, she</u> was a selfless person. <u>She</u> received great respect from the community due to her charity work. <u>Her life</u> was indeed fortunate.

(Adapted from 'Australian Identity', *Write it Right*, 1996, p. 63)

ACTIVITY 13

Text 7

<u>The sex hormone estrogen</u> is important for many physiologic processes. ‖ <u>Prolonged stimulation of breast ductal epithelium by estrogen</u>, however, can contribute to the development and progression of breast cancer, ‖ <u>and treatments designed to block estrogen's effects</u> are important options in the clinic. ‖ <u>Tamoxifen and other similar drugs</u> are effective in breast cancer prevention and treatment ‖ by inhibiting the proliferative effects of estrogen that are mediated through the estrogen receptor (ER). ‖ <u>However, these drugs</u> also have many estrogenic effects ‖ depending on the tissue and gene, ‖ <u>and they</u> are more appropriately called selective estrogen receptor modulators (SERMs). ‖ <u>SERMs</u> bind ER, ‖ (*ellipsed theme*) alter receptor conformation, ‖ <u>and</u> (*ellipsed theme*) facilitate binding of coregulatory proteins that activate or repress transcriptional activation of estrogen target genes. ‖ <u>Theoretically</u>, SERMs could be synthesized that would exhibit nearly complete agonist activity on the one hand or pure antiestrogenic activity on the other. ‖ <u>Depending on their functional activities</u>, ‖ <u>SERMs</u> could then be

developed for a variety of clinical uses, ‖ including prevention and treatment of osteoporosis, treatment and prevention of estrogen-regulated malignancies, and even for hormone replacement therapy. ‖ Tamoxifen is effective in patients with ER-positive metastatic breast cancer and in the adjuvant setting. ‖ The promising role for tamoxifen in ductal carcinoma-in-situ or for breast cancer prevention is evolving, ‖ and its use can be considered in certain patient groups. ‖ Other SERMs are in development, with the goal of reducing toxicity and/or improving efficacy.

(Osborne et al., 2000, pp. 3172–86; quoted in PubMed website, 4 September 2003)

ACTIVITY 14

Textual and interpersonal themes, as well as places where these themes are combined, are indicated in italics and brackets. Underlining indicates the extent of the theme.

Text 8

SPEAKER 1 How (*interpersonal and experiential*) do you find the local GP?‖

SPEAKER 2 Oh he's (*textual*) all right.‖

SPEAKER 1 Which (*interpersonal and experiential*)... which surgery are you at?

SPEAKER 2 Er [Name-of-Road] Street.

SPEAKER 1 [Name-of-Road] Street.

SPEAKER 2 Mm. Dr [Name-of-Doctor], he's very good ‖ but as (*textual*) I say‖we don't run to a doctor for nothing, ‖ y' know‖what I mean. ‖ But (*textual*) we've had <coughs> had us jabs for flu.‖ I got a lump on the back of my neck ‖ so (*textual*) we h+ ‖ I had to have what was it called?

SPEAKER 3 Antibiotics

SPEAKER 2 Antibiotics and (*textual*) it must have helped it to burst or summat ‖ and (*textual*) now of course it's pretty much gone. ‖ And (*textual*) that was it with me.

[...]

SPEAKER 2 I had skin cancer. ‖ I'd been digging in the garden ‖ and and (*textual*) I don't know ‖ whether (textual) I scratched myself with a <pause> ‖ 'cos (*textual*) I was doing my <pause> ‖ I don't ‖ whether (textual) a s+ a thorn caught me on the nose ‖ and (*textual*) then (*textual*) I'd been digging

SPEAKER 1 Mm.

SPEAKER 2 Cats and all sorts had been digging about, ‖ I hate cats, ‖ and (*textual*) it wouldn't heal up ‖ and (*textual*) it was going on ‖ and (*textual*) I was getting cream cream on my nose – ‖ it never ha+ healed up ‖ you see. ‖ So (*textual*) I went to the doctor's ‖ and (*textual*) they looked at it down the infirmary. ‖ Then (*textual*) they had to have those all these specialists round ‖ you you know ‖ and (*textual*) I thought, ‖ Why (*interpersonal and experiential*) the heck am I seeing other people. ‖ Anyway (*interpersonal*) they had to have ten

(Collins Cobuild Bank of English: subcorpus = brspok/UK)

Text 9

TURNIPS 'CURE SARS'

Demand for veg rockets in killer bug scare

SALES of turnips are rocketing in China‖ because (*textual*) the veg is said‖ to cure SARS. ‖

They are used in herbal remedies sold to treat severe acute respiratory syndrome. ‖

Wholesale prices of turnips in China's capital Beijing have shot up THIRTY PER CENT in a week amid fears over the deadly flu-like virus. ‖ Carrots, garlic and ginger are also included in the potions ‖ and shops have been selling out. ‖

The global death toll from SARS rose to 153 yesterday. ‖ Nine were reported in Hong Kong -the most in one day there so far. ‖ They included a woman aged 34, who died while giving birth. ‖

The condition of the baby was not known. ‖

China has been hit hardest by SARS, with 64 deaths. ‖

One newspaper in the country has recommended dead silkworms in one remedy. ‖

There is still no recognised cure for SARS, ‖ which (*textual*) has infected more than 3,300 people in at least 20 countries ‖ since (*textual*) it emerged in southern China last November. ‖

However (*textual*), a German company said yesterday ‖ it had developed a high-speed test for the virus. ‖

Artus, based in Hamburg, said ‖ it could detect SARS in two hours. ‖

Current checks can take up to ten days. ‖

Artus said ‖ it would distribute the test free to laboratories worldwide. ‖

Manager Thomas Laue said: ‖ 'It will be our share in controlling this plague.' ‖

Seven people in Britain have been treated so far for SARS symptoms. ‖

Four have recovered ‖ and (*ellipsed subject theme*) been discharged from hospital.

(Russell, *The Sun*, 16 April 2003)

Text 10

The sex hormone estrogen is important for many physiologic processes. ‖ Prolonged stimulation of breast ductal epithelium by estrogen, however, can contribute to the development and progression of breast cancer, ‖ and (*textual*) treatments designed to block estrogen's effects are important options in the clinic. ‖ Tamoxifen and other similar drugs are effective in breast cancer prevention and treatment‖ by inhibiting the proliferative effects of estrogen that are mediated through the estrogen receptor (ER). ‖ However (*textual*), these drugs also have many estrogenic effects ‖ depending on the tissue and gene, ‖ and (*textual*) they are more appropriately called selective estrogen receptor modulators (SERMs). ‖ SERMs bind ER, ‖ (*ellipsed theme*) alter receptor conformation, ‖ and (*textual*) (*ellipsed theme*) facilitate binding of coregulatory proteins that activate or repress transcriptional activation of estrogen target genes. ‖ Theoretically, SERMs could be synthesized that would exhibit nearly complete agonist activity on the one hand or pure antiestrogenic activity on the other. ‖ Depending on their functional activities, ‖ SERMs could then be developed for a variety of clinical uses, ‖ including prevention and treatment of osteoporosis, treatment and prevention of estrogen-regulated malignancies, and even for hormone replacement therapy. ‖ Tamoxifen is effective in patients with ER-positive metastatic breast cancer and in the adjuvant setting. ‖ The promising role for tamoxifen in ductal carcinoma-in-situ or for breast cancer prevention is evolving, ‖ and (*textual*) its use can be considered in certain patient groups. ‖ Other SERMs are in development, with the goal of reducing toxicity and/or improving efficacy.

(Osborne et al., 2000, pp. 3172–86; quoted in PubMed website,
4 September 2003)

Unit 10
Positioning and persuading

Prepared for the course team by Kieran O'Halloran

CONTENTS

Material required

While studying this unit, you will need:

  the course reader

  the Activities CD-ROM

  the Condordancer and Corpus CD-ROM and *Corpus Tasks*.

Knowledge assumed

You should be familiar with the following before starting this unit:

  intensifier

  interrogative

  modal finite (modal verb)

  mood

  persona

  tenor

  word frequency.

Introduction

To start this unit, look at the scene shown in the cartoon opposite.

As indicated in the cartoon, newspapers, particularly at the populist end of the market, sometimes play on fears such as the fear of losing one's job. While the actual experiential meaning of someone's words is not necessarily transformed in populist newspapers, it is common to find the interpersonal force increased. With regard to important political matters, people should ideally be given the facts as far as possible so that they can weigh them up for themselves, in this case how the facts might affect their own employment circumstances and the employment circumstances of others in their country. Being able to isolate aspects of a text that might be **positioning** readers into a particular way of seeing the world – which may be a misleading or sensationalised one – is a useful skill to possess.

IT IS EVENING TIME IN BRITAIN. A HUSBAND AND WIFE ARE RELAXING IN THE LIVING ROOM OF THEIR HOUSE. HE'S READING THE NEWSPAPER, SHE'S DOING SOME WORK FOR A PART-TIME COURSE. HE WORKS ON THE ASSEMBLY LINE OF A JAPANESE CAR COMPANY. HE HAS READ SOMEWHERE THAT THE COMPANY WAS SITED IN BRITAIN BECAUSE OF ITS SO-CALLED 'FREEWHEELING ECONOMY'. HE THINKS THIS IS SOMETHING TO DO WITH THE FACT THAT OVERSEAS COMPANIES DON'T PAY HIGH RATES OF TAX IN BRITAIN, BUT HE'S NOT REALLY SURE. AS HE READS HIS NEWSPAPER ONE HEADLINE AND OPENING SENTENCE JUMP OUT. HE READS THEM OUT LOUD TO HIS WIFE.

TWO MILLION JOBS IN PERIL. TWO MILLION JOBS WILL BE LOST IF TONY BLAIR SIGNS THE NEW EU TREATY, IT WAS FEARED LAST NIGHT.

THE EUROPEAN UNION! TREATIES! POLITICIANS! AND I VOTED FOR HIM! I'M JUST AN ORDINARY BLOKE. JUST WANT TO KEEP MY HEAD DOWN AND HOLD ON TO MY JOB. TWO MILLION JOBS WILL GO. IT SAYS SO IN THE PAPER, SO IT MUST BE TRUE.

TWO MILLION JOBS WILL GO! INCREDIBLE, DON'T YOU THINK!

BUT THEN HE REMEMBERS..

SHE DOESN'T AGREE WITH ME AS MUCH AS SHE USED TO. A FEW MONTHS AGO SHE WOULD JUST HAVE NODDED. A CHANGE HAS COME OVER HER THE LAST FEW WEEKS.

A PAUSE.. AND THEN

DARLING, IT'S SO IMPORTANT TO READ ALL OF THE STORY BEFORE MAKING A JUDGEMENT. LOOK WHAT IT SAYS HERE – THE NINTH SENTENCE DOWN.

SHE POINTS TO THE FOLLOWING

M.P. DAVID HEATHCOAT-AMORY SAID, 'WE COULD BE FACING ANOTHER TWO MILLION BRITISH WORKERS ON THE DOLE'

SHE CIRCLES THE WORD 'COULD' AND THEN THE WORD 'WILL' IN THE OPENING SENTENCE.

COULD   WILL

It is the purpose of this unit to give you some insight into how readers can be positioned by texts and to give you some skills of analysis in order to articulate how patterns of interpersonal meaning are being created. You will also see later how the use of a concordancer can help in isolating patterns of interpersonal meaning that are not so obvious when reading a text. By the end of the unit, you will be better able to maintain a critical distance from texts; that is, be better able to resist misleading positioning. Because we shall be dealing with interpersonal meanings, we are interested in the aspect of the context of situation called tenor. You came across this concept in Unit 8, where you saw that aspects of tenor can be divided into three:

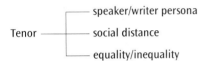

Figure 1

In Unit 8, we looked at linguistic indicators of social distance and equality/inequality. You will meet these areas again in Book 3. In Unit 8, we also examined how writers create a persona which can potentially position us into a particular interpretation. By 'persona' we mean the 'personality' of the text – something analogous to the personality of a speaker. When we listen to someone speak, we do not just listen to what they say (experiential meaning) but also to how they say it (interpersonal meaning and textual meaning). The interpersonal aspect of meaning includes how the speaker engages us. How engaged we are depends very much on how engaging their personality is. We may be engaged because we respect the speaker, or because they have authority over us, or because they are easy to be with, are charming, etc. In the same way, a text has a persona which can engage us as readers because we regard the writer as communicating with authority or because we find the writer entertaining, etc. Since we are interested in this unit in how writers position readers into potentially accepting a point of view, we shall look at speaker/writer persona in more detail.

 1 SPEAKER/WRITER PERSONA

1.1 Stance and epistemic modality

In the cartoon at the beginning of this unit, you saw that the writer of the news report (*Two million jobs in peril*) communicated certainty – marked by the use of *will* when the actual words spoken by the politician contained the less certain *could*. This commitment to a particular meaning is called the **stance** of a writer or speaker. Imagine if someone actually spoke the news-text sentence you saw earlier:

TWO million jobs <u>will</u> be lost if Tony Blair signs the new EU treaty.

What is expressed here is strong likelihood and so a strong commitment to the idea communicated – a strong stance. The person speaking is not someone who wants to engage in a debate and allow you much room for negotiation over their meaning. This persona is not so easy to negotiate with because it is rather assertive. But imagine also someone who said the following:

We could be facing another two million British workers on the dole.

Could communicates less probability, weaker commitment to the idea and so a weaker stance. The person speaking here seems less forthright. The stance allows you space to engage with the idea being presented because you are not being positioned so dogmatically. They allow you space to negotiate with their meaning; they give you space to agree or disagree. I couched the examples above in terms of a speaker persona since we tend to associate personas with people. But the written word also implies a persona (see Unit 8). In news text, this might be a conventional, institutional persona but it is a persona nonetheless. With friends of ours whom we have known for a long time, we become so used to their personas that we rather accept them for what they are. In the same way, we can get fairly inured to a news-text persona if we habitually buy only a particular newspaper title, e.g. *The Sun* or *The Times*. We may barely notice the persona any more and the special way in which it 'talks' to us.

I have drawn attention to *will* and *could*. These are what are known as modal finites and are just one way of expressing likelihood and therefore a way of expressing stance. We met them in Book 1 (they can also be referred to as modal verbs). There are other modal finites too. *May* and *might* also express likelihood, having a similar meaning to *could* in this respect. *Must* is another modal finite which can be used to express likelihood. With *must* a deduction or inference has often taken place on the basis of some evidence, e.g. *He must be at least 60. Look at all those grey hairs*. The inference made with *must* normally communicates that the speaker is fairly certain about something. You will have gathered by now that likelihood is on a continuum ranging from high to low. When a sentence expresses a degree of likelihood, we say it has **epistemic modality**. So, we could rank expressions of epistemic modality with modal finites on a continuum, as follows:

Two million jobs <u>will</u> be lost.	certainty
Two million jobs <u>would</u> be lost.	probability based on hypothetical condition
Two million jobs <u>must</u> be lost (if Tony Blair signs the new EU treaty).	deduced as fairly certain
Two million jobs <u>may</u> be lost.	possibility
Two million jobs <u>might</u> be lost.	possibility
Two million jobs <u>could</u> be lost.	possibility

You should be able to see a tight relationship between the strength of the epistemic modality, the stance created and thus the room for negotiation that the reader or hearer is given. That is, those statements with high epistemic modality (expressing certainty or strong probability) leave less room for negotiation than statements with low epistemic modality (expressing possibility).

Look at your reference grammar for more information on modal finites, their characteristics, etc. (Chapter 6, section 9 onwards).

Epistemic modality is not only expressed through modal finites, though. You will find out more in the next activity.

A CTIVITY 1 (allow about 15 minutes)

Imagine you were debating with someone and he or she made statements (a)–(k) below. In them you will see the same experiential meaning in the declarative mood being invested with different interpersonal meanings. These interpersonal meanings are achieved through modal finites and other grammatical resources which express epistemic modality. The sentences can be divided into those which position strongly and those which do not.

1   Divide the statements into two categories – those with strong positioning and those with soft positioning. The first two have been done for you. (See 'Answers to the activities' for the others.)

2   Underline the modal finites and any other grammatical resources that you have seen so far in this course that are used to communicate epistemic modality. The first two have been done for you.

(a)   Darwin's theory of evolution <u>will</u> never explain human nature.
STRONG POSITIONING

(b) Darwin's theory of evolution <u>probably</u> explains human nature.
   SOFT POSITIONING

(c) Darwin's theory of evolution would explain human nature for many people if they only knew what it was.

(d) Darwin's theory of evolution possibly explains human nature.

(e) Darwin's theory of evolution definitely explains human nature.

(f) Darwin's theory of evolution can't explain human nature.

(g) Darwin's theory of evolution might explain human nature.

(h) Darwin's theory of evolution explains human nature.

(i) It is possible that Darwin's theory of evolution explains human nature.

(j) Darwin's theory of evolution doesn't explain human nature.

(k) It is likely that Darwin's theory of evolution explains human nature.

COMMENT

The modal finites used in these statements are *will, would, can't* and *might*. Words like *definitely, possibly, probably* and *never*, which communicate meanings of epistemic modality, are known as **modal adverbs** since they modify the verbs. Adjectives which correspond to these adverbs, i.e. *definite, possible, probable,* are known as **modal adjectives** and are commonly used with **it-clauses**, as in:

Note that in your reference grammar, *modality* refers only to uses of modal verbs. In SFL, the model mainly used here, modality has this wider scope.

> It is possible that Darwin's theory of evolution explains human nature.

The use of modal markers such as *might, probably, possibly* (and also *may, could,* etc.) tells you that the speaker is prepared to negotiate to differing extents. The stance is not so assertive. The writer's persona is a reasonable one. What I mean by reasonable is that they imply that they are aware of alternative positions or that they recognise the possibility of alternative positions. You as a reader are not being positioned so strongly. By the regular use of such instances of epistemic modality, the writer can construct a persona which is **dialogic** in the broad sense of the term, i.e. not in the sense of being involved in a face-to-face conversational exchange with another speaker, but in the sense of acknowledging that whenever people speak or write they are necessarily being influenced by what has been written and spoken by others before, and that, as they speak or write, they anticipate how others are likely to respond and choose their words accordingly. By choosing certain wordings, the speaker/writer can indicate a particular stance towards other speakers/writers whereby they recognise and acknowledge alternative points of view. Equally, by choosing not to use such wordings, they can indicate a different stance – one in which they ignore, suppress or deny the validity of alternative points of view, e.g. *Darwin's theory of evolution will never explain human nature* and the other examples of strong positioning which are identified in 'Answers to the activities'.

Finally, you will have noticed from 'Answers to the activities' that there are two sentences which express strong stance even though they contain no modal finites, modal adjectives or modal adverbs. They are:

(h) Darwin's theory of evolution explains human nature.

(j) Darwin's theory of evolution doesn't explain human nature.

These are simple statements in the declarative mood with positive and negative polarity respectively.

Now that you understand something about epistemic modality, you can begin to see why it would be useful to have this knowledge. It can help you to become aware of one of the ways in which the stance of an event is reported in a newspaper. Is the stance cool and detached or it is sensationalised? As a result, this will help you to resist being positioned by the persona of a news text and thus persuaded into a particular point of view (which may indeed have little basis in fact). Looking back at the sentences from the news text, you can now say the following: low epistemic modality in David Heathcoat-Amory's statement, expressed with the modal finite *could*, has been transformed into much higher epistemic modality, as expressed by the modal finite *will*. And the headline, *Two Million Jobs in Peril*? You could say the following: verbs are commonly ellipted in headlines. Probably the easiest way for readers to link *two million jobs* and *in peril* would be as participants connected by the relational process *be*, i.e. *Two million jobs are in peril*. That is, implicit certainty in the headline is likely to be realised by the reader.

1.2 Stance and deontic modality

Epistemic modality is one type of modality that expresses stance. Let us move on to another form of modality that expresses stance. Consider the following sentence:

> MOTHER (TO CHILD) You really <u>must</u> do your homework for tomorrow's school lesson.

You can see that we have the modal finite *must*. But it is being used in a different way from *must* in *He must be at least 60. Look at those grey hairs on his head*. The latter is a deduction of probability and so an instance of epistemic modality. The former communicates *obligation* – the child has to do the homework.

Permission, obligation and necessity are also modal meanings, referred to as **deontic modality**. Again, we could rank on a continuum expressions of deontic modality with modal finites and the level of obligation as follows:

We <u>have to</u> work very hard on the grammar course.	strong obligation
You <u>must</u> work very hard on the grammar course.	strong obligation
We <u>had better</u> work very hard on the grammar course.	strong obligation
We <u>ought to</u> work very hard on the grammar course.	obligation
You <u>should</u> work very hard on the grammar course.	obligation
We <u>need to</u> work very hard on the grammar course.	necessity
We'<u>re supposed to</u> work very hard on the grammar course.	weaker obligation

See sections 6.9.2, 6.10.1 and 6.10.2 of your reference grammar for more information on modal finites (modal verbs) of obligation and necessity.

A CTIVITY 2 (allow about 15 minutes)

Imagine you were debating with someone and he or she made the statements (a) – (i) below. In them you will see the same experiential meaning being invested with different interpersonal meanings. These interpersonal meanings are achieved through modal finites and other grammatical resources that express deontic modality. The sentences can be divided into those which position strongly and those which do not.

1   Split the statements into two categories – those with strong positioning and those with soft positioning. The first two have been done for you. (See 'Answers to the activities' for the others.)

2   Underline the modal finites that are used to communicate deontic modality. The first two have been done for you.

(a)   You <u>must</u> explain why 2 plus 2 doesn't equal 5. STRONG POSITIONING

(b)   If you'<u>d like</u> to explain why 2 plus 2 doesn't equal 5, then <u>please</u> do. SOFT POSITIONING

(c)   You have to explain why 2 plus 2 doesn't equal 5.

(d)   You should explain why 2 plus 2 doesn't equal 5.

(e)   You could explain why 2 plus 2 doesn't equal 5 if you want to.

(f)   You're not supposed to explain why 2 plus 2 equals 4 but why it doesn't equal 5.

(g)   Can you explain why 2 plus 2 doesn't equal 5?

(h)   Explain why 2 plus 2 doesn't equal 5.

(i)   May I ask you to explain why 2 plus 2 doesn't equal 5?

COMMENT

With the different examples of deontic modality, it should be clear that the stance communicated positions you with more or less room to manoeuvre. An utterance like *Explain why 2 plus 2 doesn't equal 5*, which had been barked at you, might make you feel very uncomfortable. You would be strongly positioned by the deontic modality here –realised by the imperative mood. Use of the interrogative mood for the purposes of a question speech act with modal finite *can* as in *Can you explain why 2 plus 2 doesn't equal 5?* is less strongly positioning since the stance is less strong. However, *Can you explain why 2 plus 2 doesn't equal 5?* without the question intonation is more strongly positioning: it is still in the interrogative mood but the speech act is not a question, which would give the hearer room for manoeuvre, but rather a directive, a request.

1.3 Personalisation

As you will have seen from the previous activities, interpersonal meanings are often very complex. They are not only carried through the grammar of modality – deontic or epistemic – but can also be conveyed through **personalisation**, another subcategory of speaker/writer persona. This refers to whether the subjective, personal role of the speaker/writer is explicitly revealed and drawn attention to, or whether it is backgrounded, obscured or underplayed. Often the result of personalisation being made explicit in a text is that a more intimate connection is established between speaker/listener or writer/reader.

Look again at what David Heathcoat-Amory says: *We could be facing another two million British workers on the dole*. You will see that the politician uses *we* when delivering his prediction about two million British workers becoming unemployed. *We* communicates solidarity – he and his countrymen and women in Britain. But his words have been transported into a news-article context. It is possible that readers now understand that *we* includes them. That is, *we* in the news text can personalise the information for the readers, addressing the readers and taking on the inclusive sense of them and the newspaper readership. Other pronouns can potentially create strong positioning. Imagine, for instance, how you would respond in a debate on Darwin's theory of evolution if someone said the following to you:

> Surely you of all people see that Darwin's theory of evolution can't explain human nature.

This is an example of strong positioning using personalisation. The stance does not give you much room to negotiate with the statement because you are so strongly personalised. You would first have to react by asserting yourself over the speaker by drawing attention to the rhetorical use of *Surely you of all people*, even though it seems to contain some sort of compliment. Now, consider the following:

> Well, I don't know. For me at least Darwin's theory of evolution explains human nature.

The speaker is making it clear that this is their own opinion through use of the first-person pronoun. As a result, the stance gives you much more space to think about the statement and respond, to negotiate over its meaning. You have not been positioned so strongly because you have not been personalised. Personal pronouns are a common way of personalising meaning. There are other ways of personalisation which you will meet in Book 3. Finally, what you should see from this section on personalisation is that personalisation and stance often become entangled in the communication of speaker/writer persona.

ACTIVITY 3 (allow about 20 minutes)

Again imagine you are in a debate with a person who makes the statements (1) – (10) below. Consider how the personalisation in these statements together with their modality act to position you.

Decide whether these statements fall into the categories of strong positioning, medium positioning or soft positioning. The first three have been done for you (see 'Answers to the activities' for feedback).

What grammatical resources are being used to communicate the positioning?

1   Do you REALLY think Darwin's theory of evolution explains human nature? STRONG POSITIONING

2   Quite a few experts agree that Darwin's theory of evolution can't explain human nature. MEDIUM POSITIONING

3   Only a few experts hold that Darwin's theory of evolution can't explain human nature. SOFT POSITIONING

4   Darwin's theory of evolution explains our nature, don't you think.

5   There is no doubt that Darwin's theory of evolution explains human nature.

6   What's your opinion on whether Darwin's theory of evolution explains human nature?

7   What! Explain human nature with Darwin's theory of human nature? Are you crazy?

8   I am interested in whether Darwin's theory of evolution explains human nature.

9   It is most likely the case that Darwin's theory of evolution doesn't explain human nature.

10   According to the majority of Nobel Prize winners, Darwin's theory of evolution explains human nature.

COMMENT

To begin with, there is of course an element of subjectivity in interpreting statements as having strong, medium and soft positioning, especially in relation to an imagined spoken context. It all depends on the 'voices' in our heads! So you may have found that your choices of positioning strength differed slightly from mine. You may also have found this with the answers for Activities 1 and 2.

The interrogative mood (see Book 1 Unit 3) is usually associated with questions. And with a question we give our hearer or reader some space to negotiate with the proposition we are communicating. This is why there is soft positioning in (6). But interrogatives can also be used to position quite strongly, especially in concert with intensifiers such as in (1), where the intensifier is *really* or with words that carry negative meanings such as *crazy* in (7). You will notice that (4) does not have a question mark; *don't you think* has the form of an interrogative but it is not functioning as a question. Rather it is functioning to reinforce a statement and so has some positioning effect. Softer positioning can be established with use of the first person, e.g. in (8), where what is communicated is the subjectivity of the speaker. The proposition being communicated does not then sound so assertive.

Personalisation can be used to establish closeness and thus solidarity. See, for example, the use of pronouns such as *you* or *our* (4) in *our nature* instead of *human nature*. This is a very conversational way of building up intimacy. Should the listener/reader allow themselves to be positioned in this way, they would be 'on the side' of the speaker/ writer. But the possibility of persuasion does not just depend on whether we are positioned in an intimate way through use of the second person (*you*) or inclusive first person (*we/our*). Making statements *impersonal* can ratchet up the strength of the positioning (*It is most likely* in (9) and *There is no doubt* in (5)). Especially if the context is an academic one, we may be more persuaded by **impersonalisation** because of its implications of objectivity. Impersonalisation is the opposite of personalisation.

You will have noticed that I have not drawn attention to (3) and (10):

3   Only a few experts hold that Darwin's theory of evolution can't explain human nature.

10   According to the majority of Nobel Prize winners, Darwin's theory of evolution explains human nature.

According to the majority of Nobel Prize winners and *Only a few experts* are linguistic indicators of what is called **standing** – along with stance and personalisation, a subcategory of speaker/writer persona. Standing relates to laying claim to expertise or authority. *Only a few experts* does not position as strongly as *According to the majority of Nobel Prize* *winners*. But how convincing is the latter in relation to the statement *Darwin's theory of evolution explains human nature*? It relies on the prestige attached to the Nobel Prize. The Nobel Prize is awarded in six different categories – medicine, chemistry, physics, literature, peace, economics. But would we automatically want to attach great seriousness to an opinion on Darwin's theory of evolution given by a Nobel Prize winner for literature? It is important, then, to be careful with standing and to inspect the nature of the expertise being cited.

1.4 Stance and attitude

We have looked a little at three types of indicator of speaker/writer persona: standing, personalisation and stance. Stance is actually divided into two types. We have looked at one of these types of stance – modality (both epistemic and deontic). It is time to turn to the other type. This is known as **attitude** and relates to whether positive, negative or neutral meanings are being communicated. It is often realised through particular lexical choices. Let us go back to the opening of the news text we have been using in this unit to have a look at meanings of attitude:

Two million jobs in peril

TWO million jobs will be lost if Tony Blair signs the new EU treaty, it was feared last night.

Peril, *lost* and *feared* carry negative meanings. So in terms of positioning, readers have three negative values by the time they get to the end of the first sentence. Combined with the high epistemic modality of the opening sentence, the attitude helps to position the readers strongly at the start of this news article. While the use of high epistemic modality reveals a rather dogmatic writer persona, the use of the negative attitude reveals a rather alarmist one. Attitudes, especially those which characterise people, things, or situations in positive or negative terms (as good or bad, right or wrong, competent or incompetent, approved or disapproved, pleasing or displeasing, beautiful or ugly, etc.) can be highly charged interpersonally since they are the basis either on which we come together with others in communities of shared feelings and values, or by which we end up in confrontation with, or at odds with, those who hold different evaluative positions. So negative or positive values help create or destroy solidarity. For example, if you are on a short-term contract and you read the negatively attitudinally-positioned *Two million jobs in peril*, etc., then you may enter into solidarity with the message being communicated.

ACTIVITY **4**   (allow about 30 minutes)

You are going to examine the whole of the *Two million jobs in peril* news text to see the kinds of attitudinal meanings it contains. But before you do so, here is some background to the text, which comes from a British tabloid newspaper. In Britain, newspapers are, broadly speaking, divided into broadsheets and tabloids, broadsheets being the larger of the two as well as being more serious. Tabloids have a much wider circulation than broadsheets and, being less serious, contain the latest gossip about celebrities, scandals, etc. The news text you are going to read comes from the website of *The Sun* newspaper (27 May 2003, http://www.thesun.co.uk). The print version has a very large circulation of over three million readers. It thus has the potential to exert a great influence in Britain, predominantly amongst the readership which it targets. A significant issue for many years in Britain has been whether Britain would adopt the euro as its currency, making the pound redundant. The euro is the currency of the majority of countries that make up the European Union. (The European Union is a political, economic and legislative body currently consisting of 25 countries, including Great Britain. The European Commission – a seat of great power in the EU – is based in Brussels, Belgium.) There is considerable opposition to any more ceding of economic independence to the EU in certain quarters of the British press, one such newspaper being *The Sun*. The ultimate ceding of economic independence for *The Sun* would be the adoption of the euro as the currency for the UK.

(1)   Go through the text below and highlight any negative and positive attitudes (after doing this, see 'Answers to the activities'). How, in your opinion, is the writer persona trying to create solidarity with the readers and thus persuade them of the viewpoint being taken? From your analysis of attitude and personalisation, what view of British identity does the writer persona seem to want the reader to take?

(2)   Can you find examples of standing which position the reader?

Two million jobs in peril

By George Pascoe-Watson
Deputy Political Editor

TWO million jobs will be lost if Tony Blair signs the new EU treaty, it was feared last night.

A revised draft of the proposed constitution revealed that Britain would be forced to surrender control of its economy to Brussels.

And other key elements of our way of life would be affected even more drastically than first thought. The draft proved Brussels also aimed to snatch power over UK employment, foreign affairs, defence and welfare.

And it meant Britain would have to dish out generous benefits to millions of migrants from eastern Europe.

They would be allowed to flock here after ten new nations join the EU next year.

The scale of the masterplan for a United States of Europe triggered outrage last night.

Critics said booming Britain would be crippled by the sort of economic edicts that have wrecked Germany.

Tory MP David Heathcoat-Amory said: "We could be facing another two million British workers on the dole*.

"The EU will be driving our employment policies in the same direction as Germany.

"They are struggling with mass unemployment and their dole queue is rising."

Mr Heathcoat-Amory sits on the convention thrashing out the constitution but his attempts to limit its powers have been swept aside.

He backed The Sun's call for Britain to be allowed a referendum on joining the treaty.

Mr Blair has refused to stage one – although other EU states will get a vote.

A crucial phrase in yesterday's blueprint stated: "The Union shall work for a Europe of sustainable development based on balanced economic growth with a social market economy."

Experts leaped on the final three words and warned they would be a death sentence to our freewheeling economy.

Germany has laboured for years under this system which forces firms and individuals to pay high taxes which stifle growth and enterprise.

Dr Madsen Pirie, president of the Adam Smith Institute – a free market think tank – said the constitution would be disastrous for UK employment.

He said: "There is no doubt that if we were to sign up to the proposals it would result in large numbers of people being unemployed.

"The reason we are not in the bad position that most of our European partners are in is because we kept our independence from the single currency.

"This constitution would make us lose an important part of that independence.

"We absolutely must have a referendum."

Patrick Minford, professor of economics at Cardiff University, said: "This could easily put another two million on the unemployment register.

"We will bring back mass unemployment just as they have got in Germany, France and Italy."

Mr Blair will be expected to sign up to the constitution blueprint by the end of June.

[* *Dole* is informal British English for 'unemployment benefit'.]

(Pascoe-Watson, *The Sun*, 27 May 2003)

COMMENT

The writer persona is, in part, trying to create solidarity around the notion that the new European Union treaty would be bad for Britain since it would lead to mass unemployment. The writer persona is also trying to promote the view that being British involves an economic identity, e.g. the positive attitude of *booming* in *booming Britain*; *our freewheeling economy*; control of the economy being a *key element of our way of life*; *we kept our independence from the single currency*. In furthering ties with the European Union, the British economic identity of the readers of *The Sun* would be eroded.

Towards the end of the report, we have some examples of standing: *experts*; *Dr Madsen Pirie, president of the Adam Smith Institute*; *Patrick Minford, professor of economics at Cardiff University*. Minford and Pirie both use high epistemic modality in their statements on unemployment. But while their high epistemic modality statements relate to unemployment, these statements have already been preceded by a negative attitude which relates more broadly to the British *freewheeling economy*:

> Experts leaped on the final three words and warned they would be a death sentence to our freewheeling economy.

As a result, it is possible that the following can happen: the meaning of their modal statements regarding unemployment become mingled for readers of the article with the negative-attitude meanings regarding the prospects of economic integration with the EU. What the writer seems to be doing above and elsewhere is the following: to be hooking a more general anti-economic integration line onto the more specific line about impending employment gloom which all three critics refer to.

Lastly, the lack of a premodifier for *experts* in the above sentence should make the reader suspicious. The experts referred to (Madsen Pirie and Patrick Minford) are both experts in one branch of economics – free-market economics: Madsen Pirie's particular economic expertise is signalled in the text; Patrick Minford's particular economic expertise is not (although in fact his expertise is the same). We do not therefore have broad economic expert opinion in the news article. Rather, we have expert opinion on a brand of economics which the journalist (and *The Sun*) favours.

When you went to 'Answers to the activities' you may not have had exactly the same reading of attitude as me. Inevitably in detecting attitude, there is an element of subjectivity – there is no absolute objective standard for assigning positive or negative values to things. All the same, there are certain things most people would agree upon – that unemployment is a negative thing, and so on. So hopefully, in the main, you agreed with my reading.

As human beings, it can be difficult to switch off our own personal biases and predilections. It is easy to focus on aspects of a text that we immediately like or do not like and then draw conclusions on that basis. It is possible, though, that there are other aspects of a text which do not fit in with the interpretation we make. Since our interpretations can run the risk of being partial, we need to guard against our own subjectivity. A subjective interpretation would be rather limited anyway. More valuable is an interpretation that gives us an idea of how a text is likely to position readers *generally*. And to be fairly certain of this we need to be able to point to a whole host of regular patterns of meaning in a text. The more regularity of meaning we can point to, the more we can take our interpretation as having relevance for readers generally.

This is where using the concordancer can be useful. By its very nature it can point to regularities in a text that might not be so obvious to us as casual readers. Loading a news text into a concordancer reconfigures the text, reorganising it for us to see it afresh. Using the concordancer we can see regular patterns of attitude interacting with regular patterns of modality that we were not otherwise easily able to notice. The same might go for regular patterns of attitude interacting with regular patterns of personalisation. Plus, if we are used to reading a particular newspaper, we can get overused to its personas. As a result we may skip over aspects of a text that have interpersonal significance. Again, the concordancer shakes the text up, making its persona(s) more apparent. Using the concordancer may also tell us other interesting things, as we shall soon see.

❷ USING THE CONCORDANCER TO EXPLORE STANCE IN A TEXT

2.1 Finding patterns of regularity

How do we begin our search for regular patterns of meaning in a text using the concordancer? One route is to do a word-frequency list of the text. This tells you what words are common. But if you can find what the common words are in a text, this might also tell you what norms the writer is trying to establish, what patterns of stance they are trying to create in their use of a particular persona. Finally, consulting a word-frequency list frees us from the drudgery of having to count words as well as the possibility of making mistakes.

A CTIVITY 5 (allow about 15 minutes)

Have a look at the word-frequency list for the *Two million jobs in peril* news text.

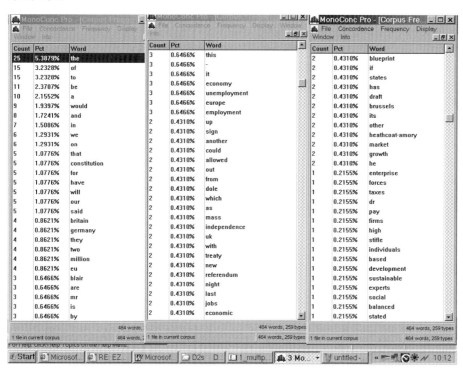

The left-hand column ('Count') shows the number of instances of a particular word. So, for example, the word-frequency list tells us that there are 25 instances of *the*. The next column ('Pct') tells us, as a percentage, the instances of a particular word in proportion to all the words in the text (464 words – as indicated at the bottom). Therefore the 25 instances of *the* constitute around 5.4% of the total number of words in the text.

On the basis that those words which are frequent might be ones that the writer is establishing positioning from, what regular patterns of meaning do you think the concordancer might make more visible?

COMMENT

Interestingly, the modal finite *would* is relatively very common. It is the sixth most common word in the text, having nine instances. It is even more common than the coordinator *and*. Another modal finite, *will*, is fairly common, with five instances. The next modal finite *could* has only two instances. Out of context, we would think of *would* and *will* as having higher modality than *could* – so their relative frequency is interesting. The article would seem to be about the strong prediction of something. But without looking at concordance lines or the text, we cannot automatically assume that meanings of high modality can be associated with all the instances of *will* and *would* or low modality with *could*. For example, *would*, *will* and *could* can also be used to make invitations, commands and requests (*Would you like to come to a party? Will you shut the window? Could you shut the window?*).

ACTIVITY 6 (allow about 15 minutes)

Overleaf you will find the concordance results for *would* and *will*. By interpreting the concordance lines, what modality do you think the writer is trying to achieve? With regard to the interpretation I made earlier of the text – of the concepts of 'unemployment' and 'economy' – what can more precisely be said now? What attitudinal meanings is *would* frequently associated with? Can you see another pattern of stance meanings that *would* is associated with?

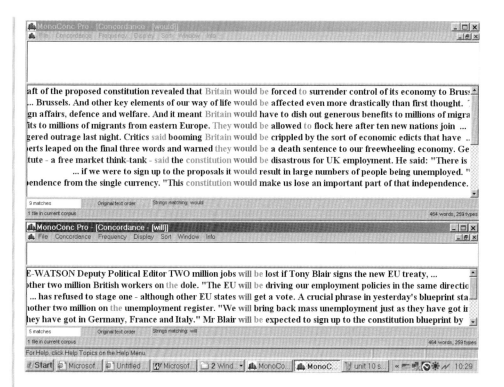

COMMENT

The meaning of *would* here relates to fairly high epistemic modality. That is, on condition that Britain signed the EU constitution, in the opinion of the journalist all of these things would happen. From the headline and the opening sentence, the news article seems to be about the dangers of signing the EU treaty for UK employment only. But now we can see quite precisely that there are, in fact, *only* two instances of a negative prediction for UK employment. Out of the other seven instances of *would*, four relate to negative predictions with high modality for the economy. That is: four instances of high modality relating to the economy against two relating more specifically to unemployment. Using the concordancer to provide this quantitative approach to the text gives support to the interpretation I gave earlier: that is, the writer is using the news text story about the impact of the signing of the EU treaty on UK unemployment to hook on a more general anti-EU perspective regarding the harm that the EU constitution would do to the economy.

But what about the other three instances of *would*? What do they refer to? One of them is a more general negative prediction for *our way of life*. The other two relate to migrants. *Britain would have to dish out* – here Britain is being obliged to do something for migrants, signalled by the deontic modal finite *have to*; and *they would be allowed to flock here* – we presumably have the prospect of the EU granting permission to migrants, signalled by the deontic modal marker *be allowed to*. So in amongst the alarmist predictions of a loss of two million jobs are other meanings which relate to deontic modality – of Britain having to support migrants financially because of an outside force: the European Union. This is something which has little to do with Britain's employment situation. I was focusing earlier on how the journalist's general concern with the British economy was being hooked on to an article which on the surface seems to be specifically about the effects of a treaty on UK unemployment. Because of this, I ended up inadvertently skipping the reference to migrants. But actually, we can go further now in the interpretation of the article. Not only does the article hook its anti-EU and anti-euro-currency politics onto a news story about the impending signing of the EU treaty and its implications for UK employment, but it also hooks its politics about immigration with a rather sensationalist line.

So we have found some patterns of meaning which seem to be sustained across the text – strong epistemic modality coupled with negative attitude and in some cases also coupled with deontic modality. Are there any other patterns which reinforce these? Let us go back to the word-frequency list to see what other words are relatively common. Let us just focus on those words that occur at least four times. Aside from certain function words such as *the, of, to, a, and, in*, and *on* which you would expect to be fairly common, we have the following: *we* (6), *constitution* (5), *for* (5), *have* (5), *our* (5), *said* (5), *that* (5), *will* (5), *Britain* (4), *EU* (4), *Germany* (4), *million* (4), *they* (4), *two* (4). Because we are interested in tenor in this unit, the relatively high number of pronouns, i.e. *we, our* and *they* is interesting. We shall feed these into the concordancer to make the lexicogrammatical environments for these pronouns more visible.

ACTIVITY 7 (allow about 15 minutes)

Look at the concordance lines for *we* and *our* in the screen shot overleaf. How do they compare with the lines for *they* from the perspective of attitude?

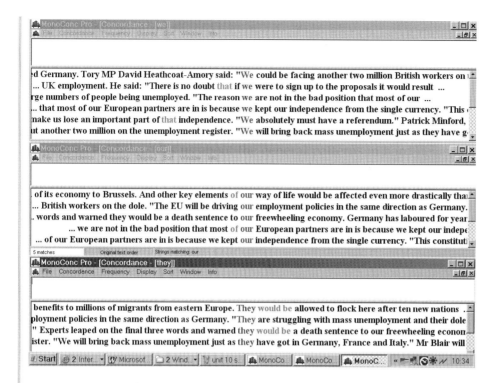

COMMENT

You should be able to see that *our* is being used to signal solidarity with certain things, for example, *our employment policies, our freewheeling economy*. Interestingly, these are things which people do not commonly feel they own or would necessarily readily identify with. I am a British national but how the British economy is run is not something that springs immediately to mind in how I would identify myself. *Our* also constructs solidarity with *way of life* as does *we*, with *we absolutely must have a referendum, we kept our independence, we are not in the bad position*.

When *they* is used, there is a negative attitude being communicated in the co-text, for example, *mass unemployment, struggling, death sentence*. There is then a clear 'us–them' basis to the text, which the concordancer makes more visible.

We have been using the concordancer to examine how patterns of lexicogrammatical meaning can be made more visible across a text. Through our use of the concordancer, we might refer to lexicogrammatical meaning as **syntagmatic** meaning. But new meanings can also be established in a **paradigmatic** way. Consider the following, again from *The Sun* (6 June 2003), about the deputy prime minister of the UK, John Prescott, who was reported to have made a rude hand gesture.

The gesture is the latest in a series of gaffes* by Mr Prescott...He has **THUMPED** a protester during an election campaign, caused a **STORM** by using two cars for a 250-yard drive, **DOZED** off at a summit and got a **SOAKING** by the pop band Chumbawumba at the Brits*.

[* *Gaffes* is a word used in British tabloids to indicate errors. *The Brits* is a pop music awards ceremony.]

(Kavanagh and Lea, *The Sun*, 6 June 2003)

Signalled by the word *gaffes*, we would understand that Mr Prescott is responsible for the actions that follow. This indeed seems to be the case as indicated in the grammar of the first three processes. *He* is the actor responsible for *thumping*, *causing a storm* and *dozing off*. A pattern of meaning has been established through these parallel structures of actor and process where the meaning established is that Mr Prescott was responsible for these gaffes. So the first three syntagmatic meanings have something in common:

He	has thumped	a protester.
He	has caused	a storm.
He	has dozed off.	
actor	process	goal

Since the syntagmatic meanings have something in common we can say that there is also a paradigmatic pattern of meaning. Consider then the other clause:

He got a soaking by the pop band Chumbawumba at the Brits.

In this incident, a member of the pop band, *Chumbawumba*, poured a bucket of water over John Prescott. The grammar of this clause clearly indicates that Prescott was not responsible for the soaking since he was the goal:

He	got a soaking	by the pop band Chumbawumba.
goal	process	actors

So this last incident can hardly be called a *gaffe*: it was not his fault that he had water poured over him. Yet the construction of this piece of text would seem to encourage the reader to think that John Prescott *was* responsible for the soaking he received. This is because a paradigmatic or vertical pattern of meaning, having been established with the first three incidents and reinforced by the word *gaffes*, seems to influence how the last incident is read.

2.2 Finding the global groove of *The Sun* text

The patterns we have just seen in this text extract on the politician, John Prescott, are local ones. This groove was fairly easy to spot given that we were dealing with such a short text fragment. But what about longer stretches or whole texts? If such a groove exists in a whole text because of regular patterns of meaning, trying to spot these patterns can be more difficult. Certainly the longer the text, the more difficult and time-consuming the spotting of patterns of regularity becomes. We know now that *The Sun* text is an obviously biased news report – but by using the concordancer we will show how to make the groove of bias in the text readily visible. By using this to find the groove, you will see how the final sentence of the report

> Mr Blair will be expected to sign up to the [European Union] constitution blueprint by the end of June

is not as neutral as it might appear. So we are not so much interested in detecting bias which can be found here and there in isolated spots in the text. We are interested rather in rendering more visible the larger organising frames of this bias in the text, which set out a groove of meaning for the reader to follow, and thus potentially funnel the reader into making a negative meaning out of this seemingly neutral portion of text.

So how do we go about finding this global groove? To investigate whether or not such a 'global' groove exists, let us go back to the word-frequency list. If we find that certain relatively high-frequency words in a text are clustered together, then we can say that there is some regularity of patterning in the text. From such observations, we might be able to see what the overall groove of the text is – the global lexicogrammatical patterning. Since it is the left-hand column which tells us where the high-frequency words are, and thus where we might more readily find cluster patterns, we shall confine ourselves to this. For the relatively high-frequency words – *the, of, a* and *and*, I found no discernible clustering and so turned to two other relatively high-frequency words: *be* (11 instances) and *would* (9 instances). Remember the concordances for *would* and *will*. If you go back to these concordances, you can see a strong clustering between *be* and *would* and between *be* and *will*, the latter also being fairly common in the text (5 instances). You should also see that the usage of *be* is in negative co-texts, a set of negative predictions. As the first few concordancer lines show us, the start of the text has a negative pattern of paradigmatic meaning: *will be lost, would be forced, would be affected*. In the seemingly neutral and rather mundane sentence:

> Mr Blair will be expected to sign up to the constitution blueprint by the end of June

we have the modal finite *will* with *be* in an expression of epistemic modality. The previous instances of *will* plus *be* and the general expressions of epistemic modality with modal finites + *be* potentially funnel reading towards a negative interpretation of this last sentence since it contains *will* + *be*. But we have only established the first part of the pattern. We also have in this sentence an infinitive, *to sign up*, a prepositional phrase realising a circumstance and containing a key word in the text, *constitution*, in *to the constitution*. Is there also evidence of a negative groove of paradigmatic meaning in the texts for these other elements?

Since *to* begins infinitives, and we need to look for evidence of negative circumstances realised by prepositional phrases beginning with *to*, we need to search for *to*. From the word-frequency list, *to* is one of the most common words in the text, with 15 instances. So that is a good start. Perhaps *to* is regularly found in negative co-texts and perhaps it clusters with other relatively common words which also are found in negative co-texts.

A CTIVITY 8 (allow about 15 minutes)

Look at the following patterns for *to*. They have been separated into infinitives and prepositional phrases. Do you find any negative patterns emerging?

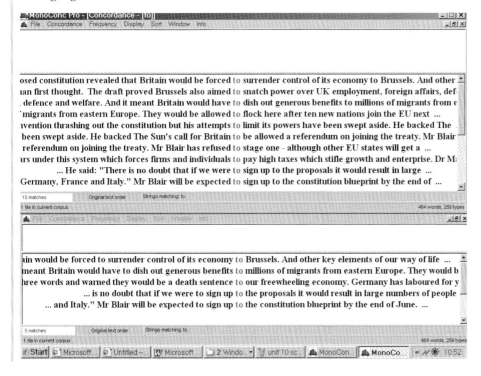

COMMENT

As with patterns we have seen before, you should see fairly negative co-texts for *to* as an infinitive as well as for the prepositional phrases.

ACTIVITY 9   (allow about 15 minutes)

Look at the concordance lines for *constitution*, another relatively common word in the text at five instances. What attitude predominantly accompanies the instances of *constitution*? What attitudes are found in the lexicogrammatical environments for the first four instances?

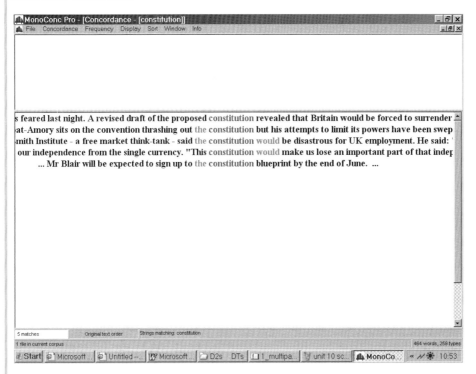

COMMENT

You should be able to see a paradigmatic pattern of meaning taking shape for the first four instances of *constitution*. Taking all this concordancer evidence together, for *be*, *will* (and the related *would*), to-infinitives and *constitution* as well as *to* in prepositional phrases realising a circumstance, we have established the text's global groove. Isolated from the text, the last sentence would appear to be an innocuous statement about what was going to happen in the future. However, coming at the end of the text, with such dense preceding negative lexicogrammatical patterning, this last sentence could position a reader to think that there are only four weeks or so before this *constitution* starts to ruin *our way of life*! We say 'position' because obviously we cannot know how the last sentence is actually read by *Sun* readers. All the same what we have done is an advance on merely pointing out lexical bias here and there in the text (e.g. *peril, crippled*). This is because the concordancer has helped us to highlight: (a) how bias is organised generally throughout the text at the lexicogrammatical level; (b) the density with which this bias is lexicogrammatically organised. As a result, the analysis went beyond isolated spotting of bias and provided some illumination of how a reader, in following this groove, could project negatively onto seemingly neutral phrases/ clauses. To reiterate, though, this analysis is only at the level of the text. How meanings are made in context by actual readers, actual *Sun* readers in this case, is another thing.

I hope you can see that the concordancer can be helpful in seeing patterns of interpersonal meanings in text, patterns that are less visible when looking at the text in its original form. I hope you can also see how useful the concordancer is in showing you how patterns of attitude and meaning can be accrued in context, patterns that are not so apparent when we go through a text word by word looking for negative or positive attitude in individual words. When you come to do your project, you may want to use the concordancer as you have been shown in this unit, particularly if your project is on news text and rhetoric. And as we have found in this unit, you should also find that the concordancer is useful in substantiating the interpretation you make of a text, substantiating it with quantitative evidence made readily available for you. More generally, I hope you have been able to see how something as apparently mundane as a newspaper text that you might just casually read through on the sofa, on the train, etc., is the result of some degree of design – design consisting of patterns of meanings which can act in mutual reinforcement to position readers into particular points of view. A few words of caution, though. Of course, not all texts are as regular in their patterning as *The Sun* text and so using a concordancer to try to find a major groove in a text may not yield sufficient evidence for that groove. Highly patterned texts such as advertisements, political speeches, prayers and certain news texts, particularly at the populist tabloid end of the market, are more likely to yield to this kind of analysis.

In Unit 8, we laid out a map of tenor (p. 31). We can now fill it in with more detail in Figure 2.

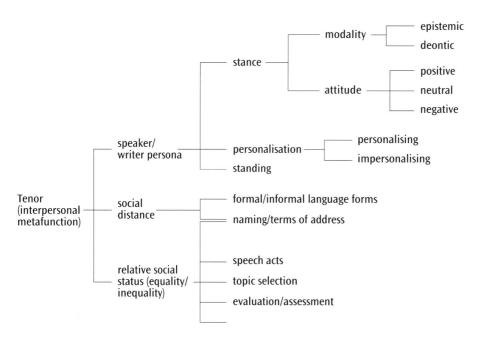

Figure 2 Map of tenor

In Unit 12 of Book 3 you will look more at issues of social distance and inequality/equality, to which you were introduced in Unit 8.

USING THE CONCORDANCER TO EXPLORE STANCE IN A CORPUS

In the previous section we used the concordancer to zoom in on a text and make the patterns of meaning across it more visible. We related this back to the text and the context since we were interested in how regular patterns of meanings can potentially position readers into accepting a particular viewpoint. But there may be occasions when we want to use a concordancer to get more of a bird's-eye view of how English is used. This could be because we are interested in addressing a particular problem that relates not so much to one text but to a particular register as used by a set of people with something in common. The reading for this unit addresses such a problem. It looks at how stance is constructed by non-native students in their academic writing through the use of it-clauses (e.g. *It is possible* in *It is possible that joining the euro currency will bring substantial economic benefits*). The clause after the it-clause, that is, the clause *that joining the euro currency will bring substantial economic benefits* is known as a **complement clause** (see your reference grammar, section 8.15.1).

Do you use it-clauses commonly in your academic writing? You probably do since they are a common way of removing the first person and so lend your writing the impression of objectivity which many disciplines require in academic writing.

The reading highlights systematically where stance meanings with this construction are often used too forcefully by non-native students; they commonly *overstate* them. This might not be too much of a problem if what is being written are popular news articles, but it could be if the writing is academic. In Chapter 6 by Hewings and Hewings (2004) in the course reader *Applying English Grammar*, you will see concordancer software used to compare a corpus of professional academic writing and a corpus of students' dissertations; this is done to see where students express stance meanings too forcefully with it-clauses. Since you yourself might be a non-native student of English, and given that you have to write assignments for this course in English, this reading should prove useful in highlighting the kinds of problems that you might face in using the resources for stance in academic English.

A CTIVITY 10 (allow about three hours)

Read Chapter 6 'Impersonalising Stance: A Study of Anticipatory "it" in Student and Published Academic Writing' by A. Hewings and M. Hewings in the course reader, *Applying English Grammar*.

While reading make notes on the following:

(1) What is an extraposed clause? (If you are still not sure after the reading, use your reference grammar.)

(2) Hewings and Hewings (2004) point out that certain adjectives are incongruous in academic text when used with *it-clauses*, for example:

> It is amazing...
>
> It is strange...
>
> It is pointless...
>
> It is wise...

Why do you think these adjectives are inappropriate with it-clauses in academic text?

(3) Why is the use of *it seems that...* inappropriate in the following two extracts?:

> In terms of training by multinationals, it seems that different studies have shown different results.
>
> In terms of employing local staff, it seems that this phenomenon is getting better nowadays because multinationals have began (*sic*) to employ a very significant proportion of local staff in managerial grades.

See what Hewings and Hewings (2004) say in their chapter.

(4) Finally, do you find the chapter helps you to understand how you use it-clauses to construct stance meanings in your academic writing? Would you say, after reading Hewings and Hewings (2004), that how you express epistemic stance in your essays is too forceful or not as forceful as you thought?

You will have an opportunity to explore how you use stance in your own academic writing in some detail, should you wish, when you come to do your project (in the *Assignment Book and Project Guide*).

Activities CD-ROM (allow about two hours)

Different grammatical traditions have different **taxonomies**, i.e. different ways of categorising language. This may be somewhat irritating, but it is a fact of grammatical life. It is, in fact, inevitable since the nature of grammatical categories is to some extent related to the purposes of the grammarian. The goals of the grammarian, as well as the 'grammatical culture' in which the grammarian finds him or herself, dictates what grammatical categories are regarded as useful. Hallidayan functional grammar is more likely to be useful to someone who needs to do close text analysis in, say, trying to ascertain ideological bias. Corpus linguists are more likely to use formal categories (e.g. noun phrase) since it is far harder to tag for functional categories. The Longman student grammar is a corpus-based grammar and so draws mainly on formal grammatical categories. Given that different taxonomies have different values and functions, it is a useful intellectual exercise to think oneself into a different taxonomy.

In this unit we have been using a taxonomy for modal verbs (modal finites) and modal resources more generally which relates to Hallidayan functional grammar. While you do many of the CD-ROM exercises, you will think yourself into the Longman taxonomy of modal verbs. Before you do the CD-ROM activities, you will need to read section 6.9 of your reference grammar to find out how it classifies modal verbs according to function. There is also some focus in this section on the form of modal verbs, e.g. the nature of semi-modal verbs. This focus will also be relevant for your completion of the CD-ROM activities.

Now work through the activities for this unit on the Activities CD-ROM.

Concordancer and Corpus CD-ROM

(allow about two hours)

Now work through the tasks for this unit on the Concordancer and Corpus CD-ROM using the *Corpus Tasks* booklet.

Conclusion

You have been able to practise and extend your skills of grammatical description, and your skills of interpreting grammatical data. You were also able to see how using a concordancer is useful in making patterns of interpersonal meaning across a text more visible. In particular, you saw the concordancer uncovering how attitudinal meanings can be accrued in co-text. I hope you have been able to see that doing this kind of exploration of stance meanings in text is fun and revealing.

Learning outcomes

After completing Unit 10, you should have developed your knowledge and understanding of:

◆ the concept of tenor

◆ how speaker/writer persona is constructed in text to position listeners/readers

◆ how concordancers can be used to explore stance in texts and corpora.

You should have developed your ability to:

◆ *describe* grammatical features of a text in relation to the concept of tenor

◆ *interpret* texts and their grammatical features with regard to tenor.

Key terms introduced and revisited	
attitude	mood
complement clause	paradigmatic meaning
deontic modality	persona
dialogic	personalisation
epistemic modality	positioning
impersonalisation	stance [modality in SFL]
intensifier	standing
interrogative	syntagmatic (meaning)
it-clause	tenor
modal adjective	taxonomy
modal adverb	word frequency
modal finite [modal verb]	

Near equivalents are given in [ ].

Answers to the activities

ACTIVITY 1

1   Strong positioning (through high epistemic modality): (a), (c), (e), (f), (h), (j).

   Soft positioning (through low epistemic modality): (b), (d), (g), (i), (k).

2   (c) Darwin's theory of evolution <u>would</u> explain human nature for many people if they only knew what it was.

   (d) Darwin's theory of evolution <u>possibly</u> explains human nature.

   (e) Darwin's theory of evolution <u>definitely</u> explains human nature.

   (f) Darwin's theory of evolution <u>can't</u> explain human nature.

   (g) Darwin's theory of evolution <u>might</u> explain human nature.

   (h) Darwin's theory of evolution explains human nature.

   (i) It is <u>possible</u> that Darwin's theory of evolution explains human nature.

   (j) Darwin's theory of evolution doesn't explain human nature.

   (k) It is <u>likely</u> that Darwin's theory of evolution explains human nature.

ACTIVITY 2

1   Strong positioning (through high deontic modality): (a), (c), (d), (f), (h)

   Soft positioning (through low deontic modality): (b), (e), (g), (i)

2   (c) You <u>have to</u> explain why 2 plus 2 doesn't equal 5.

   (d) You <u>should</u> explain why 2 plus 2 doesn't equal 5.

   (e) You <u>could</u> explain why 2 plus 2 doesn't equal 5 if you want to.

   (f) You're not <u>supposed to</u> explain why 2 plus 2 equals 4 but why it doesn't equal 5.

   (g) <u>Can</u> you explain why 2 plus 2 doesn't equal 5?

   (h) Explain why 2 plus 2 doesn't equal 5.

   (i) <u>May</u> I ask you to explain why 2 plus 2 doesn't equal 5.

ACTIVITY 3

Strong positioning: 1, 5, 7, 10.

Medium positioning: 2, 4, 9.

Soft positioning: 3, 6, 8.

ACTIVITY 4

Negative attitudes are highlighted in colour; positive attitudes are underlined.

Two million jobs in peril

By George Pascoe-Watson
Deputy Political Editor

TWO million jobs will be lost if Tony Blair signs the new EU treaty, it was feared last night.

A revised draft of the proposed constitution revealed that Britain would be forced to surrender control of its economy to Brussels.

And other key elements of our way of life would be affected even more drastically than first thought. The draft proved Brussels also aimed to snatch power over UK employment, foreign affairs, defence and welfare.

And it meant Britain would have to dish out generous benefits to millions of migrants from eastern Europe.

They would be allowed to flock here after ten new nations join the EU next year.

The scale of the masterplan for a United States of Europe triggered outrage *last night.*

Critics said booming Britain would be crippled by the sort of economic edicts that have wrecked Germany.

Tory MP David Heathcoat-Amory said: "We could be facing another two million British workers on the dole.

"The EU will be driving our employment policies in the same direction as Germany.

"They are struggling with mass unemployment and their dole queue is rising."

Mr Heathcoat-Amory sits on the convention thrashing out the constitution but his attempts to limit its powers have been swept aside.

He backed The Sun's call for Britain to be allowed a referendum on joining the treaty.

Mr Blair has refused to stage one – although other EU states will get a vote.

A crucial phrase in yesterday's blueprint stated: "The Union shall work for a Europe of sustainable development based on balanced economic growth with a social market economy."

Experts leaped on the final three words and warned they would be a death sentence to our freewheeling economy.

Germany has laboured for years under this system which forces firms and individuals to pay high taxes which stifle growth and enterprise.

Dr Madsen Pirie, president of the Adam Smith Institute – a free market think tank – said the constitution would be disastrous for UK employment.

He said: "There is no doubt that if we were to sign up to the proposals it would result in large numbers of people being unemployed.

"The reason we are not in the bad position that most of our European partners are in is because we kept our independence from the single currency.

"This constitution would make us lose an important part of that independence.

"We absolutely must have a referendum."

Patrick Minford, professor of economics at Cardiff University, said: "This could easily put another two million on the unemployment register.

"We will bring back mass unemployment just as they have got in Germany, France and Italy."

Mr Blair will be expected to sign up to the constitution blueprint by the end of June.

(Pascoe-Watson, *The Sun*, 27 May 2003)

Unit 11
The angle on the world

Prepared for the course team by Kieran O'Halloran and Peter White

CONTENTS

Materials required

While studying this unit, you will need:

> your reference grammar
> the course reader
> the Activities CD-ROM.

Knowledge assumed

You should be familiar with the following before starting this unit:

> circumstance
> clausal circumstance
> marked theme
> nominalisation
> object
> participant
> passive
> process
> subject
> subordination
> thematisation
> theme.

Introduction

> Fishermen traditionally caught 100,000 tons of fish per year in the North Sea.

> The North Sea used to provide 100,000 tons of fish per year.

Above are two ways of representing the same thing. Certain things are included in the first sentence which are not in the other and vice versa. In the first, you can see that there is an action initiated by the participant, *fishermen*, and that the natural world is represented in a circumstance, *in the North Sea*. In the second sentence, we have a representation in which humans are not made explicit, and the natural world is not relegated to the role of circumstance.

Different representations. So what? Just different ways of talking about the same thing. Does it matter? Do we need to pay attention to such differences? Yes. The reason why it is important to do so is because grammatical representations are often linked to different ways of viewing the world, and thus to our mental habits. The first sentence could be seen to reveal a view of the world wherein humankind operates on Nature, where Nature is somehow separate or distinct from humankind. Such a perspective, reinforced by this kind of grammatical representation, would help to legitimise our domination of Nature, taking its 'resources' from it. Nature is just a 'place' where we get things we need. But this domination has come at a price. Rather late in the day, we are becoming more aware that exploitation of Nature has knock-on effects on ecosystems – and ultimately knock-on effects for us. The North Sea cannot provide us with so much fish any more (because it has been overfished and time has not been given for fish to spawn). In the UK the price of cod, for example, has increased significantly.

Representations which place Nature in a focal position instead of us, and which get away from the idea that we dominate Nature, just using it for our own ends – the view of many, certainly in the West – may help us to change our mental habits with regard to the natural world. Reading the first representation, we may be led to ask questions such as: Why don't fishermen catch so much fish any more? Is it something to do with the fishing industry? Are there fewer fishermen these days? Reading the second representation, we are more likely to ask Nature-focused questions rather than human-focused ones, such as: What's the problem with the North Sea? Why doesn't it yield so much fish any more? In doing so, we can change our mental habits – the assumption that Nature is something to be dominated and consumed without our having to worry about the effects of this domination and consumption.

In Unit 8 you saw the aspect of situation known as field and its associated linguistic metafunction, the experiential. In drawing attention to the two representations above, I have been dealing with experiential meaning and the **angle of representation** of two versions of the same event, angles of representation which emphasise one thing over another and thus in the process avoid mention of certain things. In this unit we will focus on experiential meanings, i.e. meanings linked to different representations and thus different understandings of the world of human experience. While in Unit 9 we looked at how experiential meanings are packaged, in this unit we will look at how experiential meanings can be emphasised or avoided. The various meanings in a text do not necessarily have the same impact. Certain meanings are likely to have more impact than others because of the way the text is constructed and because as readers we tend to assume that how the text is constructed is relevant to what we should focus on. The purpose of this unit is to attune you better to how meanings can be emphasised and avoided in a text through its angle of representation.

❶ EXPERIENTIAL CONSTITUENTS: A RECAP

Because we are dealing with experiential meaning in this unit, let us begin by recapping on the experiential constituents that we saw in Book 1 relating to the aspect of situation known as field. In the context of meanings by which we reference and interpret the world of experience, we saw that the functional linguistic approach identifies three main constituents of language which represent the world:

◆ Participants – typically expressed by chunks organised around noun phrases and acting to identify entities in some experiential world.

◆ Processes – typically expressed as chunks organised around verb phrases and acting to identify happenings and states of affairs in some experiential world.

We have come across the following processes: material (e.g. *kick, hit, catch*), mental (e.g. *think, see, wonder*), relational (e.g. *is, have*) and verbal (e.g. *say, explain*). A process may be made up of a verb complex, e.g. *used to provide* in *The North Sea used to provide 100,000 tons of fish per year*.

◆ Circumstances – typically expressed as adverbial phrases or prepositional phrases and acting to provide some context for the participants and processes.

Later in this unit, we will be identifying different types of participant for different types of process. This will help you to become more sensitive to the experiential meanings in text.

I said at the start of the unit that we would be looking at how representations can avoid talking about something. What we shall see in the next section is how grammatical representation allows us to make connections between things in the world or to avoid making these connections altogether.

CONNECTIONS IN THE WORLD: MAKING OR AVOIDING THEM IN TEXT

A CTIVITY 1 (allow about 10 minutes)

Look at the following opening to a news text. Look at the processes underlined (one in the headline). Think about the participants connected with these processes. What do you notice about the number of participants around the two processes? How does this affect how the event is being construed in grammar?

Bullets <u>wreck</u> Blair visit

FOUR people were wounded in a gunfight between political extremists and police about 100 yards from Tony Blair in Cape Town yesterday after officers spotted men handing out guns to demonstrators baying for the Prime Minister's blood.

Mr Blair's convoy of cars had been held up by the demonstration organised by a group calling itself Against Global Oppression, and he was smuggled in through a side entrance of the Castle moments before shooting <u>broke out</u>.

The police said that they had seen two men distributing arms to protesters who held up placards condemning the British and American airstrikes against Iraq and saying 'Death to Blair', 'One Blair, one bullet'.

(Adapted from Kiley and Sherman, 1999, p. 1)

COMMENT

It is common for processes to involve two participants. For example, there are two participants in the clause *Bullets wreck Blair visit* – *Bullets* and *Blair visit*. Two-participant clauses of this type, where there is an interaction between the participants, are described as **transitive** – there is some 'transition' from one participant to another. With *Bullets <u>wreck</u> Blair visit*, the first participant brings about the process. *Bullets <u>wreck</u> Blair visit* is then transitive. For the reader of the text, an explicit connection between entities in the world (e.g. *bullets*) and another entity (*Tony Blair*) is understood. Generally, transitives indicate that one participant acts upon, targets or interacts with a second participant in some way. Since the concept of transitivity applies only to participants which interact with one another, the notion only applies to material, mental and verbal processes. There may be two participants around the relational process *is* in *John is happy* but there cannot be said to be interaction between *happy* and *John*. On the other hand, with participants around a material process (*John kicked the ball*), a mental process (*John watched the play*), or a verbal process (*John told a story*), clearly there is interaction between participants.

It is also possible for clauses to involve just one participant:

Shooting (*participant*) broke out (*process*).

We call such one-participant clauses intransitive. Since there is just the one participant, there can be no 'transition' from one participant to another. Use of the **intransitive** verb, to *break out*, enables the journalist to avoid making a connection between shooting and who actually did the shooting or got shot. Intransitive structures avoid making explicit connections between entities in the world, and thus we do not see who or what is responsible for the event. Here are some more examples:

Twelve people died in a fire. (But who is responsible for starting the fire and thus the deaths?)

The building fell down. (Was it the wind? Was it built correctly?)

The demonstrators rioted. (Did the demonstrators decide to riot or were they incited to riot by an external agent, e.g. the police?)

To sum up: experiential meaning in clauses may involve connections being made between participants in the world; or such connections may be deliberately avoided. Choices of transitive or intransitive structure enable the writer or speaker to place emphasis on these connections in text or to avoid them in text.

As we saw in Unit 8, the metafunctions – experiential, interpersonal and textual – are entwined with one another. So whether something is transitive or intransitive may be because it is also serving one, two or all of these metafunctions.

A CTIVITY 2 (allow about five minutes)

With regard to the textual metafunction, can you say why the author of the news text in Activity 1 may have chosen to use the intransitive structure *shooting broke out*?

C OMMENT

FOUR people were wounded in a gunfight between political extremists and police...before shooting broke out.

By the time the reader gets to *before shooting broke out* they already know something about this incident – *four people were wounded*, and there was a *gunfight between political extremists and police*. Because the reader knows these points, subsequent mention of the incident does not need to be very long. Otherwise they may become bored in being fed details they already know. General cues are all that are required. This explains the brevity of *shooting broke out*. But how is this brevity achieved? *Shooting* is a nominalisation (see Unit 9) which is necessarily more reduced than a participant – process – participant structure (e.g. *X shot 4 people*). *Broke out* being an intransitive structure has only one participant (*shooting*) rather than two. So the fact that *shooting* is an intransitive also contributes to the brevity required.

Identifying intransitive processes can be tricky because, unlike *broke out* in the Blair text, they are often followed by chunks of language which may seem at first glance to be participants but are in fact circumstances. Indeed, intransitive clauses may include one or more circumstances, in addition to the one participant. For example:

> *Ordinary civilians* (*participant*) sheltered (*process*) <u>behind an ornamental wall</u> (*circumstance – location*).
>
> *The teargas canister* (*participant*) suddenly (*circumstance – how*) exploded (*process*) <u>among the crowd</u> (*circumstance – location*) with a huge bang (*circumstance – in what manner*).

Similarly, many transitive clauses contain one or more circumstances, in addition to their two participants. For example:

> *The police* (*participant*) were firing (*process*) *teargas* (*participant*) <u>into the air</u> (*circumstance – where/in what direction*).
>
> *Officials* (*participant*) had brought (*process*) *him* (*participant*) <u>through a side entrance</u> (*circumstance 1 – location*) moments earlier (*circumstance 2 – when*).

A CTIVITY 3   (allow about 30 minutes)

You are now going to practise identifying transitive and intransitive processes. In the following sentences, first identify participants, processes and circumstances, including the type of circumstance in each case. (In this unit it will be important to feel confident in identifying circumstances.) Then indicate whether the clause is transitive or intransitive. The first two have been done for you.

(*Pa* = participant, *C* = circumstance, *Pr* = process)

1   Suddenly, reporters heard the crack of shotguns in the streets.

   <u>Suddenly</u>, (*C – in what way*), *reporters* (*Pa*) heard (*Pr*) *the crack of shotguns* (*Pa*) in the streets (*C – location*). [Transitive]

2   The police fired wildly at demonstrators.

    The police (Pa) fired (Pr) <u>wildly</u> (C – *in what way*) at demonstrators (C – *location*). [Intransitive]

3   The protesters were demonstrating against Britain's role in the recent airstrikes.

4   Rounds of birdshot injured three people severely.

5   Police used strong-arm tactics against the protesters.

6   The British prime minister was attending an awards ceremony.

7   Police also used rubber bullets, stun-grenades and teargas.

8   They were vigorously brandishing threatening placards.

9   Police used apartheid-era security laws against the demonstrators.

10   A smaller demonstration at the airport passed off peacefully.

See 'Answers to the activities' for feedback.

You now know that intransitives can enable the writer to avoid making a direct connection between entities in the world. So in the clause *shooting broke out*, we only have one participant – *shooting*. With just this clause, we do not know who is affected in the shooting. Of course, in context, we would know from the first sentence that four people had been wounded. But what about who did the shooting? Clearly, in the fragment *shooting broke out* we do not know who was responsible. And when we go back to the first sentence for more context:

> FOUR people were wounded in a gunfight between political extremists and police...

we still do not know who was responsible. We do not know who the **actor** participant is. This is because a different grammatical construction has allowed the actor to be removed.

A CTIVITY 4 (allow about five minutes)

What type of grammatical construction in *Four people were wounded* enables the actor to be removed?

COMMENT

As you know from Book 1, the first clause above is in the passive voice. There are, in fact, two types of passives: **long passives** and **short passives**. A long passive is where two participants are present as in:

| The demonstrators | were shot | by the police. | LONG PASSIVE |
| participant | process | participant | |

Note that the second participant is normally signalled with *by*. A short passive is one where the second participant in the active voice is not included, as in:

The demonstrators	were shot.	SHORT PASSIVE
participant	process	

Here are some more short passives where the actor is not included:

The cakes are being cooked.

Violence has been provoked.

The vase had been broken.

Short **passivisation** enables the removal of actors, and hence is another way of avoiding representing connections in the world. So the exclusion of the actor in the opening sentence of the Blair text, through passivisation as well as the use of the nominalisation *shooting* and the intransitive *break out*, means that responsibility for the action is absent at the start of the text. In Section 5, you will get some practice in identifying short passives. (You can also read about long and short passives in your reference grammar section 6.6.)

It is common in news for the passive voice to have a textual metafunction in allowing the removal of the actor because we can readily understand who the actor is. That is, the short passive can avoid communicating information that we would know already, we can easily infer, or is irrelevant, e.g. *This bridge was built in 1878 (by a team of engineers and builders)*. Because when we read, we bring a whole swathe of background knowledge to bear on the text, this enables us to fill in gaps by making inferences. On the common avoidance of actor participants in news, here is what your reference grammar has to say (p. 168):

> News is similar to academic writing in using the passive voice to make the agent [actor] less prominent. Often the focus of a news story is an event that involves a person or institution. The agent [actor] may be easy to guess or unimportant...It is natural in such cases to omit agents [actors] and use the passive voice. For example, reference to 'the police' is omitted in the following:
>
> Doherty was arrested in New York in June. (NEWS)
>
> In other cases, the actors may not be known, or they cannot be mentioned for legal reasons:
>
> The officer was beaten and repeatedly kicked in the head. (NEWS)

If we go back to the Blair text, to the opening clause *Four people were wounded ...* , we see that with *wounded* we are not able to infer an actor as we can with the above examples. *Wounding* is not prototypically associated with a particular type of actor in the same way that *arrest* is prototypically associated with the police. With *wounding*, it is difficult to infer an appropriate actor.

❸ ANGLE OF REPRESENTATION

So far we have looked at how connections between entities in the world can be avoided or highlighted. But text may give prominence to certain experiential meanings not just because it includes them: they can also be emphasised because of the way the text is structured, in turn leading readers to a particular interpretation. In what follows, we will go back to the opening of the Blair text to highlight how the organisation can affect experiential meaning. That is, we will look at how organisation of the text might lead the reader to make certain assumptions about how the event took place. Here is the opening of the Blair text again, divided into its sentences:

Bullets wreck Blair visit

1 FOUR people were wounded in a gunfight between political extremists and police about 100 yards from Tony Blair in Cape Town yesterday after officers spotted men handing out guns to demonstrators baying for the Prime Minister's blood.

2 Mr Blair's convoy of cars had been held up by the demonstration organised by a group calling itself Against Global Oppression, and he was smuggled in through a side entrance of the Castle moments before shooting broke out.

3 The police said that they had seen two men distributing arms to protesters who held up placards condemning the British and American airstrikes against Iraq and saying 'Death to Blair', 'One Blair, one bullet'.

A CTIVITY 5 (allow about 20 minutes)

After you read the headline and the first sentence, did you think Tony Blair was in danger? When you read the second sentence, did you revise your opinion? In terms of text organisation, can you account for why the first sentence might lead to the assumption that Mr Blair was in danger?

COMMENT

When we read, we tend to assume that texts are constructed in such a way that we can derive relevant meanings without having to make too much effort. So it is natural for us as readers to make meaningful connections between participants and circumstances. Furthermore, at the start of a news text we do not have very much information and so we make assumptions which may turn out to be false. Newspapers commonly exploit the fact that initially we have to do a lot of 'filling in', and commonly guide us into deriving dramatic meanings which turn out to be misleading.

So with the headline *Bullets wreck Blair visit*, we might initially assume that Tony Blair had been fired at. In this transitive clause, the *Blair visit* has been wrecked by bullets – it has been seriously affected. Since *bullets* is the actor of this wrecking, *Blair visit* is what is called the **goal** participant. When we go on to read sentence (2), we see that Tony Blair was not directly fired at, but we might make the assumption that he was in danger. How is sentence (1) constructed so that we might arrive at such an inference? In that sentence, we have the following set of circumstances:

> in a gunfight between political extremists and police (*circumstance – how*)
>
> about 100 yards from Tony Blair in Cape Town yesterday (*circumstance – place*)
>
> after officers spotted men handing out guns to demonstrators baying for the Prime Minister's blood (*clausal circumstance of time*).

(To review clausal circumstances, see Book 1 Unit 6.)

The circumstance of place – *about 100 yards from Tony Blair* – is fairly specific about how close Blair was to the gunfight. I said earlier that readers assume textual information is relevant and as a result naturally make meaningful connections between participants and circumstances without too much effort. So in the absence of information from sentence (2) – that Blair was inside a castle – it is likely that readers will assume from sentence 1 that there was no set of walls between the *bullets* and Blair and that as a result he was in danger.

In sentence (2), information about Blair is made the focus (*Mr Blair's convoy of cars*). From a textual point of view, Mr Blair is part of the theme (see Unit 9) of sentence (2). You may remember from Unit 9 that the theme is the first chunk of meaning in a clause up to and including an experiential element. The theme here is *Mr Blair's convoy of cars*. Making Tony Blair part of the theme of sentence (2) keeps the focus on him and thus may influence the reader to 'drag' the inference that they may have made – that Tony Blair was in danger – into their reading of sentence (2). In other words, the possible inference that Blair was in danger can be sustained through the thematisation of *Blair* in the second sentence. All of this is in line with the common interpersonal functions of the headline and the opening sentence or two in news texts to try to 'hook' the reader into the article through dramatising the event being reported.

◆4 OPENING OF THE BLAIR TEXT: WHY IS IT ORGANISED IN THE WAY IT IS?

I have given a functional interpretation of the opening of the Blair text and how it could initially mislead readers into making the event seem more dramatic (for British readers especially), thus creating a greater likelihood of the news text being read. It is useful to explore alternative texts to see if we can ascertain more specifically why the text construction can mislead the reader in the way it does. Why does the Blair text work when other versions would not work so well? We saw that the opening of the Blair text could be said to have been constructed in line with the emphasis that the opening of news text places on the interpersonal function – to hook the reader in. Presumably its construction is in line with ease of understanding as well. Perhaps also there are other communicative functions associated with the news register which impact upon the construction of the Blair text. Could there be conventions of usage associated with news production which impinge upon the construction of the opening to the Blair text?

A CTIVITY 6 (allow about 40 minutes)

Consider the three following alternative versions of the original text, (1), (2) and (3) below. With regard to the functions of news text, why do you think these did not appear?

(1) Bullets wreck Blair visit

After officers spotted men handing out guns to demonstrators baying for the Prime Minister's blood, four people were wounded in a gunfight between political extremists and police about 100 yards from Tony Blair in Cape Town yesterday.

(2)   Bullets wreck Blair visit

About 100 yards from Tony Blair in Cape Town yesterday after officers spotted men handing out guns to demonstrators baying for the Prime Minister's blood, a gunfight between political extremists and police led to four people being wounded.

(3)   Bullets wreck Blair visit

A gunfight between political extremists and police led to four people being wounded about 100 yards from Tony Blair in Cape Town yesterday after officers spotted men handing out guns to demonstrators baying for the Prime Minister's blood.

Here is the original to enable you to compare:

Bullets wreck Blair visit

FOUR people were wounded in a gunfight between political extremists and police about 100 yards from Tony Blair in Cape Town yesterday after officers spotted men handing out guns to demonstrators baying for the Prime Minister's blood.

C OMMENT

Why versions (1) and (2) do not work

In (1) and (2) the circumstantial information holds up the reader's processing. This is in conflict with what is called the principle of **end-weight** (see your reference grammar, p. 400). English prefers long and complex elements to be placed at the end of a clause and thus after the main verb, so as to make understanding of the sentence easier. If the sentence is initially 'top-heavy', as in (1) and (2), it places a heavy burden on the reader, who has to keep a lot of information in short-term memory before reaching the main verb. (Note: because there is no easy way of producing an immediate visual record of what speakers say in a conversation which they can reflect on, and because there is limited planning time, it is not surprising that the principle of end-weight is especially adhered to in conversation.) Through comparison, we can see that the original text adheres to the principle of end-weight since the main verb, *were wounded*, comes very early in the opening sentence.

A problem with beginning with such subordination in (1) and (2) (see Book 1 Unit 6 on subordinate clauses) is that the beginning of each sentence contains a lot of new information. Ordering of information is typically from **given** to **new**. Given information is related to previous information, and new information is taken up in what follows in the text. This order of information makes it easier for receivers to understand, because the clause starts with something familiar.

This flow from given to new is known as the **information-flow** principle (see your reference grammar, p. 399) and it contributes to the cohesion of the text. For example, in the original version we know from the headline that bullets are involved. So, at the beginning of sentence (1), we are readily able to relate *bullets* to *wounding*, which comes very early in the text. From the perspective of information flow, the original works better than versions (1) and (2).

The factors just outlined – end-weight and information flow – relate to ease of processing. But there are other factors affecting the organisation of the original Blair text – ones that relate to the conventions of news production. Consider in the Blair text, for example, the clausal circumstance with *after* as a subordinator. Looking at the Longman corpus evidence, we find the following:

> Compared with other registers, news is particularly marked in its use of *after*, where it often provides background information about prior events, following presentation of the main story line:
>
> (1) *In a related case, four Trinity College Dublin student leaders were cleared of contempt* **after the society sought to have them jailed for alleged breaches of an earlier injunction restricting distribution of literature on abortion services.** (NEWS)
>
> (2) *A Coroner's comments have goaded health bosses into issuing new guidelines* **[after a mentally handicapped woman died [after fracturing her skull]].** (NEWS)
>
> (3) *Teenager Matthew Brown is being hailed as a hero for saving a toddler from drowning* **after the child plunged into a fast-flowing stream.** (NEWS)
>
> [...]
>
> *He abandoned the attack* **after the woman screamed and bit him several times.** (NEWS)
>
> (Biber et al., 1999, p. 844)

Indeed, the use of *after* as a subordinator in news is marked in relation to other registers:

each ▪ represents 200

	CONV	FICT	NEWS	ACAD
after	▪	▪▪	▪▪▪▪	▪

Figure 1 *After* as a common circumstance adverbial subordinator across registers; occurrences per million words (Biber et al., 1999, p. 844)

Since Biber et al. (1999, p. 844) flag up the use of *after* as providing background information following presentation of the main storyline, this use of *after* in news would commonly be located in the first or second sentence of a news text. But since the clause with *after* as subordinator provides background information after presentation of the main story line, we would not expect it to be overly emphasised in the opening sentence either. We would not expect it to come first. This would also be a reason for ruling out text (1).

You may have noticed in the examples above that the *after* clausal circumstances in Biber et al. (1999) are associated with negative scenarios. Similarly, you should be able to see that following *after* in the Blair text is also a negative situation:

> after officers spotted men handing out guns to demonstrators baying for the Prime Minister's blood.

It seems that negativity is associated with *after* clausal circumstances in news. Given that the focus of news is often on tragic events, this is not really surprising.

Why version (3) does not work

(3) Bullets wreck Blair visit

A gunfight between political extremists and police led to four people being wounded about 100 yards from Tony Blair in Cape Town yesterday after officers spotted men handing out guns to demonstrators baying for the Prime Minister's blood.

We have seen why alternatives (1) and (2) would probably not be considered as an acceptable presentation of events that would sell newspapers. But what about version (3)? From its headline, we know that guns are involved in this incident – clearly, bullets come from guns. *A gunfight* as the theme of the opening clause is not really new information: in fact it constitutes given information, and conforms to the information-flow principle. Most of the information in the fragment comes after the main verb, *led to*, so (3) is not really in conflict with the end-weight principle either. Furthermore, the clausal circumstance with *after* as subordinator does not come first in (3). Why, then, is the original still preferable?

From what Biber et al. (1999) say, clausal circumstances in news with *after* as subordinator usually come after presentation of the main storyline. We therefore need to decide which version presents the main storyline. One way of ascertaining this is to look at a corpus of news texts and find out what grammatical features are associated with the presentation of the main storyline. The Longman corpus of news texts tells us that the short passive is commonly used for reporting actions in the news register. Biber et al. (1999, p. 479) list the following verbs as occurring over 40 times per million words of news in the passive:

> *be* + accused, announced, arrested, beaten, believed, charged, delighted, hit, injured, jailed, killed, named, released, revealed, shot, sold.

You may have noticed that many of these verbs carry negative connotations. As with our examination of *after* above, this should not be too surprising given that the field of hard news relates to tragedies, disasters, murders, wars, etc. To clarify the notion of hard news (and how it is distinguished from soft news), here is Bell (1991, p. 14):

> Newsworkers' basic distinction is between hard news and features. Hard news is their staple product: reports of accidents, conflicts, crimes, announcements, discoveries and other events which have occurred or come to light since the previous issue of their paper or programme. The one-off, unscheduled events such as fires and disasters are sometimes called 'spot news'. The opposite to hard news is 'soft' news, which is not time-bound to immediacy. Features are the most obvious case of soft news. These are longer 'articles' rather than 'stories' covering immediate events. They provide background, sometimes 'editorialize' (carry the writer's personal opinions), and are usually bylined with the writer's name ... For both newsworkers and researchers, the boundaries between hard and soft news are unclear ... journalists spend much of their energy trying to find an angle which will present what is essentially soft news in hard news terms. Journalists and media researchers both recognize hard news as the core news product, the typical against which other copy will be measured. Hard news is also the place where a distinctive news style will be found if anywhere.

A short passive and a verb that carries negative connotations – *Four people were wounded* – are what we have in the original Blair text. Passivisation enables the goal to be thematised and passivisation will, given the above, commonly operate in news on a verb associated with something negative. Thus it becomes apparent why the original version opens with *Four people* as a thematised goal participant with the (negative) verb *wound* in the passive voice. This explains why version (3) is not the original even though it is not in conflict with the end-weight and information-flow principles. On the rationale that the participant who is negatively affected is likely to be the theme of the opening sentence in a news report, if there are two or more participants who have been negatively affected, we can deduce that the participant who has been most negatively affected is the most likely to feature as the theme of the opening sentence. While the reader will know from the headline that the story relates to Tony Blair, all of the above explains why *Tony Blair* is not the theme of the first clause of the original text. Incidentally, it is another reason why version (2) does not work so well.

Making comparisons with corpus evidence, as above, gives us some idea of why a particular news text is likely to be constructed in the way it is. The corpus evidence tells us about the general patterns in hard news reporting and we can look to see if the particular text shares the general patterns of the corpus. If this is the case, we may be able to say we are dealing with a 'prototypical instance' of the register. The opening of the Blair text conforms to some extent with the grammatical arrangements of prototypical hard news texts. A word of caution, though: Biber et al. (1999) were specific about *after* in relation to the main storyline and thus to the register of hard news rather than journalism in general. The Longman news corpus contains soft news as well as reviews, etc. As a result, Biber et al. (1999) should be treated carefully in relation to how they might provide information on what is prototypical about hard news.

⑤ ACTORS, GOALS, INTRANSITIVES AND TRANSITIVES

A CTIVITY 7 (allow about 10 minutes)

Another prototypical aspect of a hard news report is a concentration on actions. To help you recall some of the treatment of processes in Unit 5 of Book 1, can you say which of the processes underlined in the following fragment from the Blair text are material processes, and which are not?

Bullets <u>wreck</u> Blair visit

FOUR people <u>were wounded</u> in a gunfight between political extremists and police about 100 yards from Tony Blair in Cape Town yesterday after officers <u>spotted</u> men <u>handing out</u> guns to demonstrators <u>baying for</u> the Prime Minister's blood.

Mr Blair's convoy of cars <u>had been held up</u> by the demonstration <u>organised</u> by a group calling itself Against Global Oppression, and he was <u>smuggled</u> in through a side entrance of the Castle moments before <u>shooting</u> broke out.

The police <u>said</u> that they <u>had seen</u> two men <u>distributing</u> arms to protesters who <u>held up</u> placards <u>condemning</u> the British and

American airstrikes against Iraq and <u>saying</u> 'Death to Blair',
'One Blair, one bullet'.

C OMMENT

The material processes, in their lexeme form, are: *wound, wreck, hand out, bay, organise, smuggle, distribute, hold up.*

You can see, for example in *shooting broke out,* that processes are not only realised by verbs, but also by –ing forms (*shooting*).

The non-material processes, also in their lexeme form, are: *spot, see, say, condemn.*

Different processes have different participant types. We have already seen the participant types for material processes – actor and goal. It is important to understand that actors are not necessarily subjects and goals not necessarily objects. Consider the following material process from the Blair text:

subject	
Mr Blair's convoy of cars	had been held up.
goal	material process

You will notice that the above example is in the passive. As a result the subject corresponds to the goal. The active-voice version would make the actor correspond to the subject and the goal to the object:

subject		object
The demonstration	held up	Mr Blair's convoy of cars.
actor	material process	goal

So whether a subject is an actor or a goal depends on whether the sentence is active or passive.

A CTIVITY 8 (allow about 40 minutes)

You will now practise identifying actors and goals, and consolidate your knowledge of transitives and intransitives. On the next two pages is the complete Blair text. Go through it and identify all the intransitive material-process clauses, i.e. where there is an actor in the subject position but no goal.

The text is first presented in its original form to enable easy reading. However, do not use this version for your analysis; use the second version, which has been slightly modified to facilitate analysis. The text has been divided into clauses with the sign ||. This is used to indicate clause boundaries within clause complexes, either between coordinated clauses or main and subordinate clauses. Double square brackets, [[ ]], indicate embedded clauses. (See Book 1, Unit 6 for information on subordinate clauses, embedded clauses, etc.) Where some element of the clause is understood rather than explicitly stated (for example, in non-finite dependent clauses where the subject is not actually present in the clause but is carried over from the main clause) then that 'understood/carried over' element will be indicated in curly brackets{}. For example, if the original had been

> The police opened fire on the protesters and then formed a solid defensive line

it will be presented for analysis as:

> The police opened fire on the protesters || (*clause division*)
> and then {the police} (*ellipted subject*) formed a solid defensive line.

Remember that you should only consider clauses which involve material processes, and which have been underlined. (Ignore any clauses which are not underlined.)

The original version follows – the version formatted for analysis follows after.

Bullets wreck Blair visit

FOUR people were wounded in a gunfight between political extremists and police about 100 yards from Tony Blair in Cape Town yesterday after officers spotted men handing out guns to demonstrators baying for the Prime Minister's blood.

Mr Blair's convoy of cars had been held up by the demonstration organised by a group calling itself Against Global Oppression, and he was smuggled in through a side entrance of the Castle moments before shooting broke out.

The police said that they had seen two men distributing arms to protesters who held up placards condemning the British and American airstrikes against Iraq and saying 'Death to Blair', 'One Blair, one bullet'.

The officers said that they gave the crowd five minutes to disperse before firing teargas and throwing stun grenades at the demonstrators. They then opened fire after being shot at themselves.

Officers took deliberate aim with shotguns loaded with lightweight birdshot as others armed with automatic rifles crouched with their weapons at the ready. But Superintendent Wicus Holtzhausen said the police did not use sharp-point ammunition.

Two members of People Against Gangsterism and Drugs – a vigilante group with its own armed wing – were arrested: a man who had been wounded in the neck and shoulder and a woman grazed on the head by a bullet.

A child was also seen being carried away from the scene, and a reporter running for cover was caught in the crossfire and shot in the legs by a police gun.

Ordinary civilians fled the scene and dived for cover behind an ornamental wall as the demonstrators, some of them women wearing long dresses, attempted to hide their firearms.

Mr Blair ignored the pandemonium on the street and continued with his programme, presenting British soldiers with medals for their work in retraining the South African Army. But members of his entourage said that they heard the gunshots and the sounds of police and ambulance sirens wailing through the city.

(Kiley and Sherman, 1999, p. 1)

Analysis version

(1)   Bullets wreck Blair visit

(2)   FOUR people were wounded in a gunfight between political extremists and police about 100 yards from Tony Blair in Cape Town yesterday ‖

(3)   after officers spotted [[(4) men handing out guns to demonstrators [[(5) {demonstrators} baying for the Prime Minister's blood.]]]]

(6)   Mr Blair's convoy of cars had been held up by the demonstration [[(7) {demonstration} organised by a group [[(8) {the group} calling itself Against Global Oppression,]]]] ‖

(9)   and he was smuggled in through a side entrance of the Castle ‖

(10)   moments before shooting broke out.

(11)   The police said ‖

(12)   that they had seen [[(13) two men distributing arms to protesters]] ‖

(14)   who {protesters} held up placards [[(15) {placards} condemning the British and American airstrikes against Iraq ‖ (16) and saying 'Death to Blair', 'One Blair, one bullet'.]]

(17)   The officers said ‖

(18)   that they {the police} gave the crowd five minutes ‖

(19)   {in order for the crowd} to disperse ‖

(20)   before {the police} firing teargas ‖

(21)   and {the police} throwing stun grenades at the demonstrators.

(22)   They {the police} then opened fire ‖

(23) after {the police} being shot at themselves.

(24) Officers took deliberate aim with shotguns [[loaded with lightweight birdshot]] ‖

(25) as others [[armed with automatic rifles]] crouched with their weapons at the ready. ‖

(26) But Superintendent Wicus Holtzhausen said ‖

(27) the police did not use sharp-point ammunition.

(28) Two members of People Against Gangsterism and Drugs – a vigilante group with its own armed wing – were arrested: ‖

(29) a man who had been wounded in the neck and shoulder ‖

(30) and a woman grazed on the head by a bullet.

(31) A child was also seen being carried away from the scene, ‖

(32) and a reporter [[(33) {a reporter} running for cover]] was caught in the crossfire ‖

(34) and {a reporter was} shot in the legs by a police gun.

(35) Ordinary civilians fled the scene ‖

(36) and {ordinary civilians} dived for cover behind an ornamental wall

(37) as the demonstrators, << (38) some of them women wearing long dresses >>, attempted to hide their firearms.

(39) Mr Blair ignored the pandemonium on the street ‖

(40) and {Mr Blair} continued with his programme,

(41) {Mr Blair} presenting British soldiers with medals for their work in [[(42) {British soldiers} retraining the South African Army.]]

(43) But members of his entourage said ‖

(44) that they heard the gunshots and the sounds of [[(45) police and ambulance sirens wailing through the city.]]

An interrupting clause is placed between << >>.

See 'Answers to the activities' for feedback.

Having isolated the nature of one-participant clauses we now move on to look at two-participant clauses. As we saw earlier, under another set of options it is possible to represent such processes as involving two participants. As you will know by now, there are two grammatical structures by which two-participant actions can be depicted: transitive clauses and long passives. For example:

Transitive

King Alfred (*actor*) cooked (*process*) the cakes (*goal*).

The thieves (*actor*) broke (*process*) the vase (*goal*).

The police (*actor*) provoked (*process*) the violence (*goal*).

Long passive

The cakes (*goal*) were cooked (*process*) by King Alfred (*actor*).

The vase (*goal*) was broken (*process*) by the thieves (*actor*).

The violence (*goal*) was provoked (*process*) by the police (*actor*).

It is necessary to note that while transitives and long passives are similar in that they both depict the process as involving two participants (an actor and a goal), they are significantly different in other important aspects with respect to their communicative functionality and effect. They are different in terms of the informational emphases and the focusing they provide. As you know, passivisation enables the object of an active sentence to be thematised.

The notion of 'long passive' was introduced in Section 2 but we did not discuss its grammar. We should note that there is another significant aspect of the grammar of the long passive. In the transitive option, the actor is expressed by means of just a noun phrase – for example, *King Alfred*, *the thieves*, *the violence*, etc. However, in the long passive there is a rather different arrangement, involving a prepositional phrase beginning with *by* – hence *by King Alfred*, *by the police*, etc. Here a noun phrase is present, but only as one element in a longer structure, that of a prepositional phrase – hence in this case the actor role is expressed via the structure *by* + noun phrase (e.g. *by* + *King Alfred*; *by* + *the police*). You will probably remember that the typical arrangement in English grammar is for all participants (including actors and goals) to be expressed by means of noun phrases and for circumstances to be realised either by prepositional phrases or by adverbs. Thus, the following would be typical of the grammar:

My grandmother (*participant = noun phrase*) used to cook (*process = verb phrase*) the *cakes* (*participant = noun phrase*) in an old gas oven (*circumstance = prepositional phrase*: in + an old gas oven).

From this perspective there is something grammatically atypical about the long passive. Here the actor role is being realised by a structure – a prepositional phrase – which elsewhere is associated with circumstances and not with participants. Accordingly, there is something ambiguous about the grammatical status of, for example, *by the police*, or *by King Alfred*. From the perspective of grammatical structure, these formulations look more like circumstances than participants. Remember that circumstances are typically more marginal or peripheral to the grammar of the clause. They add background information which is not required for a meaningful or grammatical utterance. On the other hand, there do seem to be semantic grounds for classing such formulations as actors (and hence as participants), on the grounds that the by-phrase (*by police, by King Alfred*) in the long passive carries the same informational value as the actor in the active-voice equivalent. Thus in both *Alfred cooked the cakes* and *The cakes were cooked by Alfred* there is a clear indication of who caused or initiated the action. As a consequence, while we may still choose to class such passive by-phrases as actors, we need to note that they are grammatically unusual, that there is something about the grammar of such formulations which may present such actors as in some way less central to the action, as to some degree a more marginal element in the event being described.

◢ CTIVITY 9 (allow about 30 minutes)

1   Go back to the analysis text set out in Activity 8 on pp. 159–160. This time identify all the transitive and long-passive material-process clauses as well as the actors and goals. Once again you should confine yourself to the material-process clauses (remember that they are indicated by underlining).

2   Now return to the analysis text and identify any instances of such short/agentless passives in the indicated material process clauses. Return to Section 2 if you need to remind yourself what short passives are.

See 'Answers to the activities' for feedback.

⬢ OTHER TYPES OF PARTICIPANT

You were asked at the start of Section 5 to identify all the material processes in the opening of the Blair text. I indicated the non-material ones – *spot, see, say, condemn*.

◢ CTIVITY 10 (allow about five minutes)

Can you group these non-material processes into two broad groups in terms of meaning? You may want to return to Unit 5 to refresh your memory on different non-material-process types.

COMMENT

You should have found that the verbs *spot* and *see* go together because they relate to the sense of sight. These sense verbs are a subcategory of mental processes. Since mental processes include the process of thinking/cognition (*think, believe, know, expect, decide, plan, understand*), of sensing/perception (*hear, see, notice, smell*), of feeling/emotion (*love, fear, desire, please, anger, frighten*) it would be inappropriate to refer to participants associated with these processes as actors or goals. We do not really 'do' something when we *fear* something, for example. Rather, you could say we 'experience' fear. And, appropriately, the participants associated with mental processes are called **experiencer** and **experience**.

Officers	spotted	men handing out guns.
experiencer	mental process	experience

Since *to spot* is a mental process (i.e. a different process from a material process), it has different participants. The experiencer is the participant who is sensing, feeling, perceiving, etc. (this participant is also known as the **senser**). The thing that is being sensed, felt, etc. is the experience (also known as the **phenomenon**). The experience does not have to come after the experiencer and may be the theme of the clause. For example:

Her dancing	amazed	me.
experience	mental process	experiencer

Mental processes will be accompanied by one or two participants depending on whether the verb is being used transitively or intransitively. Moving on, you may have grouped the verbs *say* and *condemn* together as verbal processes because they relate to speech generally. Naturally, being a different process to material and mental processes, verbal processes have different participant types. These are **sayer** and **verbiage**:

They	said	yes.
sayer	verbal process	verbiage

'Sayer' refers to who or what is responsible for the verbal process and 'verbiage' to what is said. Some verbal processes are explicit as to who receives the communication. This participant is known as the **receiver**:

They	told	him	a story.
sayer	verbal process	receiver	verbiage

You will meet verbal processes and sayers again in the reading accompanying this unit. There are no relational processes in the early part of the Blair text. Just to remind you, these are processes that describe, identify or indicate possession/association. Relational processes are thus concerned with some relatively fixed condition or state of affairs. For example:

Julia Roberts	is	a beautiful woman.
token	relational process	value

In Unit 20 of Book 4, a fifth process type, *existential*, is used in analysis. Here such processes are included under relational processes.

Since we have a relational process, and not a material or a mental process, we must have different participant types. In the above clause, realised with a relational process, the person or thing being described is known as the **token**. The participant of the clause which provides the description is known as the **value**. We will come across tokens and values in the reading. Just to reiterate a point made in Section 2, the transitive/intransitive distinction does not apply to relational processes. This is because there is no interaction or transition between participants in relational processes.

❼ EMPHASISING PROCESS AND PARTICIPANT TYPES IN FICTIONAL TEXT FOR EFFECT

We have concentrated on a news text in this unit and related it, to some extent, to corpus findings associated with news. We turn now from news to fiction. In this section, we will look at an extract from a short story in relation to the different process and participant types we have just looked at. We will be particularly interested in material processes and mental processes as well as their associated participant types. As the figures from Biber et al. (1999, p. 366) show, material processes are very common in all four registers. Mental verbs are also quite common but markedly more common in fiction and conversation than in news and academic prose. The high frequency of mental processes in conversation reflects the communicative purposes of that register: talking about what people think or feel. Since, in conversation, speakers operate online (and thus have little or no time for planning), they tend to rely on relatively few verbs. In the LSWE corpus the following words for mental processes are the most frequent in conversation, at over 2,000 occurrences per million words: *see, know, think, want, mean*.

Fiction has communicative purposes similar to those of conversation, reporting the physical activities of fictional characters together with their thoughts, feelings and speech. In contrast to conversation, the LSWE fiction corpus shows greater lexical diversity and less repetition in choice of verbs. Naturally, authors of fiction have greater opportunity for careful production. And since fictional texts are often valued for their aesthetic aspects, this frequently results in a more varied selection of verbs. All the same, the LSWE corpus indicates that the three mental verbs that are very common in conversation – *see, know* and *think* – are the most common mental verbs in fiction. These three verbs, as in the conversation corpus, occurred over 2,000 times per million words of fiction. If we are asked to characterise the field of fiction, one of its dimensions would probably be that it explores the mental life of characters. This would seem to be borne out by the frequency of the verbs of cogitation – *know* and *think*. The frequency of *see* would also point to perception by characters being a large part of the field of fiction.

We are going to look at a piece of fiction. Below is an excerpt from a short story by Ernest Hemingway (1899–1961) called 'Big Two-Hearted River: 1' (1924) from the collection *The Essential Hemingway* (1980, pp. 344–5). To give you some background: Nick – the character mentioned – is setting up camp on his own. As you will read in line (3) below, he is very hungry and wants to establish camp before he cooks. Good authors allow readers to imagine characters and to be involved with what they are doing. A common dictum in how-to-write-a-story books is *Show, don't tell*: do not tell the readers about the mental state of a character; show them indirect evidence, as this will engage the imaginings of the readers more. Analysis of process types and participant types can highlight how an author indirectly shows the mental state of a character.

A CTIVITY 11 (allow about 40 minutes)

While you are reading the Hemingway extract below (which is divided into sentences), consider the following questions.

(1) What can the process types and associated participant types that Hemingway emphasises tell you about the mind-set of the character Nick? The processes have been underlined below.

(2) In relation to the LSWE corpus evidence of common types of mental processes, what conclusions might you draw about what Hemingway is trying to emphasise regarding Nick's mental life?

(3) Think also about the thematisation of the extract. Does the choice of thematisation support your response to questions 1 and 2? Is there anything else about the grammar of the text that supports your interpretation?

    1   The ground <u>rose</u>, wooded and sandy, <u>to overlook</u> the meadow, the stretch of river and the swamp.

    2   Nick <u>dropped</u> his pack and rod-case and <u>looked for</u> a level piece of ground.

    3   He <u>was</u> very hungry and he <u>wanted to make</u> his camp before he <u>cooked</u>.

    4   Between the two jack-pines, the ground <u>was</u> quite level.

    5   He <u>took</u> the axe <u>out</u> of the pack and <u>chopped out</u> two projecting roots.

6   That <u>levelled</u> a piece of ground large enough <u>to sleep on</u>.

7   He <u>smoothed out</u> the sandy soil with his hand and <u>pulled</u> all the sweet fern bushes by their roots.

8   His hands <u>smelled</u> good from the sweet fern.

9   He <u>smoothed</u> the uprooted earth.

10   He did not <u>want</u> anything <u>making</u> lumps under the blankets.

11   With the axe he <u>slit off</u> a bright slab of pine from one of the stumps and <u>split</u> it into pegs for the tent.

12   He <u>wanted</u> them long and solid to hold in the ground.

13   With the tent <u>unpacked</u> and <u>spread</u> on the ground, the pack, <u>leaning</u> against a jack-pine, <u>looked</u> much smaller.

14   Nick <u>tied</u> the rope that <u>served</u> the tent for a ridge-pole to the trunk of one of the pine trees and <u>pulled</u> the tent <u>up</u> off the ground with the other end of the rope and <u>tied</u> it to the other pine.

15   The tent <u>hung</u> on the rope like a canvas blanket on a clothes line.

16   Nick <u>poked</u> a pole he <u>had cut up</u> under the back peak of the canvas and then <u>made</u> it a tent by <u>pegging out</u> the sides.

17   He <u>pegged</u> the sides out taut and <u>drove</u> the pegs, <u>hitting</u> them down into the ground with the flat of the axe until the rope loops <u>were buried</u> and the canvas <u>was</u> drum tight.

COMMENT

There is one dominant process type in the extract – material. Nick is presented as frequently acting physically on concrete objects: (2), (5), (6), (9), (11), (14), (17).

What is communicated is the impression of a person who is keenly concentrating on the task (presumably because of his hunger), someone who is resourceful and well-practised at setting up camp. The accumulation of material processes indicates a methodical, structured approach to the task. This interpretation is supported by the smaller number of mental processes:

3   He was very hungry and he <u>wanted to make</u> his camp before he cooked.

10   He did not <u>want</u> anything making lumps under the blankets.

12   He <u>wanted</u> them [bright slabs of pine] long and solid to hold in the ground.

(*Looked for* in sentence (2) – *Nick dropped his pack and rod-case and* <u>looked</u> *for a level piece of ground* is closer to a material process since it suggests

Nick is actively searching. *Wanted to make* in sentence (3) is a mental process realised as a verb complex. Although this verb complex has the verb *make* in it, which suggests action, what is being expressed is a mental idea about action – hence a mental process. Finally, sentence (8), *his hands smelled good from the sweet fern* is a relational process.)

The much smaller number of mental processes would seem to suggest that Nick wants to get on and complete the setting up of camp. He has not got time for mental reflection, taking in the scenery (scenery is mentioned only in sentence (1)). Comparison with the LSWE corpus evidence for mental processes also supports this line. In this extract, we do not have the verbs *see*, *think* or *know*. Of course, fiction writers are free to use a variety of mental verbs! But the preponderance of *see*, *think* and *know* in the corpus tells us that visual perception and mental cogitation are things that show up commonly in fiction. This is not surprising in that fiction keys us into the mental life of its characters. While 'prototypical fiction' would seem to be concerned with exploring the interior life of characters (i.e. their cogitations and perceptions), on the basis of the corpus evidence the fact that Hemingway does not use these verbs or other verbs with related meanings reinforces Nick as a 'man of action' at this time. Paradoxically, the lack of mental processes of cogitation or perception (and the preponderance of material processes) does indeed tell us something about his interior life!

There are no verbal processes (Nick is on his own after all) and there are very few relational processes. For example:

3   He <u>was</u> very hungry and he wanted to make his camp before he cooked.

4   Between the two jack-pines, the ground <u>was</u> quite level.

Sentence (3) describes Nick's state. After this point, there are no further attributes used to describe Nick, e.g. *happy*, *sad*, *hungrier*. Again, this would seem to indicate he is focused on one thing.

The constant thematisation of *he* or *Nick* also helps emphasise the methodical staging of the task. We know from sentence (1) that Nick is beside ground that is wooded; there is a meadow, a river and a swamp. But there are no circumstantial themes introducing a mental process, such as in:

<u>Across the river</u>, Nick could see herons...

to indicate Nick was taking his mind off the task.

It is very common for subjects to be themes. But in sentence (11) there is a circumstantial theme:

With the axe	he	<u>slit off</u>	a bright slab of pine...
circumstantial theme	actor	material process	goal

Since *with the axe* is not the subject, this is a marked theme (see Unit 9). In this case we have a circumstance that indicates how Nick was able to slit off the pine. But this marked theme contributes very much to the logical order that Nick brings to the task. You need an axe in your hand before you can start chopping off slabs of pine. So the marked theme here is not in conflict with the overall interpretation.

Finally, the combination of clauses is quite simple. There is little or no elaboration through use of subordinate clauses. Much of the linking of clauses is through coordination. Again this supports the interpretation that Nick is methodical and gets on with the task without wasting time – the task being a set of subtasks. (See Book 1 Unit 6 for information on coordination, subordination, clause complexing, elaboration, etc.)

In general we understand the hard news register (e.g. the Blair news text we have been focusing on in this unit) without too much effort. This is because of the existence of normal contextual conditions for communication. In these contextual conditions, there is a straightforward channel of communication from addressor to addressee – in this particular case from news reporter to newspaper reader. Our reading purpose is to take in the new information the writer is reporting. However, with a piece of fiction, we do not have such a straightforward channel of communication. Hemingway was not writing for a particular audience and as a result the normal contextual conditions for communication do not apply.

The very detachment of a piece of fiction from normal contextual conditions has the effect of focusing the reader's attention on the language itself and projecting the reader into the 'world' that the author creates. Since there will be variation in the way that different readers project into fiction, there is unlikely to be only one interpretation of a piece of fiction. You may well have a different interpretation from mine. However, this also does not mean that 'anything goes' – that any interpretation is as good as any other. While interpretations will vary because we are different people and project differently into fictional writing, some interpretations will be more or less convincing than others because they do or do not provide enough justification through close description of the text, description which involves different 'angles' of analysis whose results support one another.

The interpretation I gave of the Hemingway fragment was not exhaustive since the description was not exhaustive either. But to reach the above interpretation there were references not only to the experiential function but to the textual function and corpus evidence – all angles of analysis whose results supported one another. As you have seen in the analysis of the Blair text and the Hemingway short story extract, any interpretation should receive support from as many different angles as possible as well as from different sources, for example, corpus evidence.

Summing up types of participants

Let us now sum up the different types of participant in a table.

Process	Meanings	Participants	Example
material	actions, events	actor, goal	Jim (*actor*) hits Joe (*goal*).
mental	perception, emotion, thought	experiencer, experience	Tom (*experiencer*) saw Jim (*experience*).
verbal	speaking, writing	sayer, receiver, verbiage	Paul (*sayer*) told Mindy (*receiver*) a story (*verbiage*).
relational	existence, states, relationships	token, value	John (*token*) is sick (*value*).

8 EMPHASISING NATURE THROUGH GRAMMAR

From an extract which showed a character who does not have time to ponder on Nature, we ourselves now move to a discussion, via the reading for this unit, of how Nature is construed through grammar.

ACTIVITY 12 (allow about 15 minutes)

You may remember the following two sentences from the opening of this unit:

> Fishermen traditionally caught 100,000 tons of fish per year in the North Sea.

> The North Sea used to provide 100,000 tons of fish per year.

Using the terminology for participant types introduced in this unit, and the terminology on thematisation introduced in Unit 9, explain (with more precision than the opening of this unit did) how the representations differ, and thus how the different representations can be seen as being bound up with different angles on Nature.

COMMENT

The reading for this unit is from Chapter 11 by Andrew Goatly (2000) in the course reader, *Applying English Grammar*. The chapter endorses an ecological perspective, that human technological domination is resulting in potentially serious implications for the planet. This technological domination of Nature – where humans act on Nature – Goatly refers to as the *technological world-view*. He contends that this world-view is often reflected in transitive clauses. In the following:

> Fishermen traditionally caught 100,000 tons of fish per year in the North Sea

there is a division into actors who apply force or energy (*fishermen*) and the inert or passive goal (*fish*). This might make us think of the fish as inactive, as though cause and effect only operate in one direction. Secondly, this sentence marginalises the 'environment' or location circumstance (*in the North Sea*), suggesting that the North Sea is either powerless or is not affected. In fact, the catching of so many tons of fish obviously changes the North Sea's ecosystem.

Goatly argues instead that grammatical representation should reflect an ecological world-view where humans and nature are interrelated. Such grammatical representation would sensitise us more to the fact that we cannot just act on Nature or take from Nature without expecting consequences for the planet. For example, our burning of carbon-based fuels has resulted in the greenhouse effect, which in turn has led to increasing global warming.

Here now are some ways Goatly suggests in which technological world-view representations can be grammatically modified in order to emphasise the interrelatedness of humans and Nature. As you will see below, such grammatical modification has both a textual and an experiential function.

Using grammar to sensitise the reader towards an ecological perspective

1 Activating a location circumstance as actor

Instead of marginalising the environment by referring to it in a location circumstance, we have the option of turning it into a subject where it is a theme and so receives more emphasis. So with:

Fishermen	caught	100,000 tons of fish	in the North Sea.
actor	material process	goal	circumstance

by transforming the location circumstance into an thematised actor, we can produce a sentence that sensitises the reader towards an ecological perspective:

The North Sea	used to provide	100,000 tons of fish.
actor	material process	goal
theme		

To emphasise that it is Nature which provides resources for humans, a **recipient** or **beneficiary** participant type could be added, i.e. *us* human beings in:

The North Sea used to provide us with 100,000 tons of fish per year.

2 Activation of experiences

We can reconstruct experiences in mental-process clauses as though they were actors in material processes. For example:

I	saw	the river.
experiencer	mental process	experience

→

The river	arrested	my gaze.
actor	material process	goal

Similarly:

I love the forest. → The forest gives me a lift.

Experiences can also be thematised with intransitive structures:

I saw the river. → The river came into view.

3 Activation of tokens

Relational processes can be transformed into material ones so that instead of Nature being static, it is seen as active. For example:

Five trees	are	in the valley.
token	relational process	value

→

Five trees	stand	in the valley.
actor	material process	circumstance

Similarly:

There is a boulder on top of the hill. → A boulder tops the hill.

A CTIVITY 13 (allow about 30 minutes)

To enable you to practise 'changing world-views', here are some exercises. For each section there are ten transformations. The first five require you to change from a technological world-view to an ecological one. In the technological world-view, humans and their actions are either explicit or they are implicit through words such as *crop* or *fertilised*. The remaining five require you to transform an ecological representation into a technological one. A verb is given for you to base the transformation on and the first one is done for you in each case.

See 'Answers to the activities' for feedback.

A1   Technological to ecological world-view through activation of location circumstance

Circumstance of location → actor (in material process clause)

1   American consumers get two-thirds of their fruit from the orchards of California. (→ supply)

Californian orchards <u>supply</u> American consumers with two-thirds of their fruit.

2   Several million people live on the prairies of North America. (→ support)

3   Traditional herbalists and their patients obtain useful remedies from the tree bark. (→ benefit)

4   Children pick berries off the bushes. (→ succour)

5   The wheat crop finds nourishment in the nitrates of the legumes planted the previous year. (→ nourish)

A2   Ecological to technological world-view

Actor (in material process clause) → circumstance of location

6   Organically fertilised rice fields enabled a twofold increase in production. (→ was possible)

A twofold increase in production <u>was possible</u> in organically fertilised rice fields.

7   The areas where snakes had been introduced caused a reduction in the rat population. (→ came about)

8   The monsoon rain relieved the drought-stricken crops. (→ recover)

9   These islands can assist the overspill of human population from the mainland to survive. (→ survive)

10   The coast of Oman can help the fishermen to continue to live. (→ live)

B1   Technological to ecological world-view through activation of experience participants

Experience in mental process → actor (theme) in material process

1   I concentrated on the eagles for three hours. (→ held)

The eagles <u>held</u> my concentration for three hours.

2   I noticed the glow worms. (→ caught)

3   I worried about the coming hurricane. (→ disturb)

4   I looked intently at the birds. (→ held)

5   I perceived the sudden movement in the undergrowth. (→ attract)

B2 Ecological to technological world-view

Actor (theme) in material process → experience in mental process

6   The waterfall riveted his gaze. (→ observed)

     He <u>observed</u> the waterfall intently.

7   The trek through the rainforest pleased me. (→ like)

8   The seashore delighted the children. (→ enjoy)

9   The snakes disgusted her. (→ hate)

10   The name of the species of monkey escaped her. (→ forget)

C1 Technological to ecological world-view through activation of tokens

Token in relational process → actor in material processes

1   Jordan is to the West of Iraq. (→ lies)

     Jordan <u>lies</u> to the West of Iraq.

2   The mountain is above the village. (→ rear up)

3   The lake is at the foot of the mountain. (→ sit)

4   The path is beyond the wood. (→ runs)

5   The river was long. (→ stretch)

C2 Ecological to technological world-view

Actors in material processes → tokens in relational process (there are no prompts in this part)

6   The chasm gaped.

7   The crevasse yawned ahead of them.

8   The city sprawls.

9   The mountain dominates the valley.

A CTIVITY 14 (allow about three hours)

Read Chapter 11 'Nature and Grammar' by Andrew Goatly in the course reader, *Applying English Grammar*.

In the reading, Goatly investigates the grammatical differences in the representation of Nature between William Wordsworth's poem *The Prelude* (1850) and a corpus of all the articles in one edition (2 May 1996) of *The Times* of London (written by staff writers). Both case studies are of comparable length. Goatly addresses two specific questions in his case study:

(1)   What elements of Nature figure most prominently in *The Times* compared with *The Prelude*?

(2)   What degrees of power do *The Times* and *The Prelude* confer on Nature?

To answer the first question, the Concorder computer program was used to compile a frequency-list of all the vocabulary in the two texts which referred to the following classes of natural objects:

◆ animals
◆ plants, flowers, fruit, vegetables
◆ landscape
◆ rivers, lakes, seas, and other bodies of water
◆ weather.

Once this was done, the second research question could then be addressed. For all the clauses in which this Nature vocabulary occurred, whether as participants or circumstances, a Hallidayan analysis of processes and participants was conducted. This type of analysis Halliday calls a **transitivity analysis** – analysing clauses to find out what the type of process is and what the types of participants are. Note that the idea of transitivity is not the same as looking at clauses to see if they are transitive or intransitive.

Before you begin the chapter from 'Nature and Grammar', here are some tasks to make your reading more focused:

(1)   While reading Goatly's case study, make brief summaries of the differences in grammatical representations of Nature in *The Prelude* and *The Times* that Goatly reports.

(2)   How do the grammatical modification techniques outlined just before Activity 13 show up in *The Prelude* so that its representations of Nature are in line with the 'ecological perspective'?

(3)   Goatly mentions **ergative verbs**. Why does he favour ergative verbs for representing Nature? Why might ergative verbs be suited to transforming a sentence that reflects a technological world-view into one that reflects an ecological one?

COMMENT

(1) In *The Prelude*:

♦ Nature is represented as twice as powerful as in *The Times*.

♦ Weather and animals are the most powerful natural elements, just as they are in *The Times*.

♦ Rivers are frequently represented as sayers, in contrast to *The Times*.

♦ Mountains and landscape feature as transitive actors, which never happens in *The Times*.

♦ Natural actors figure intransitively without goals, more so than in *The Times*.

(2) In *The Prelude*:

♦ Experiences are activated into actors, especially in conjunction with terms of address: the experience of Nature is very powerful.

♦ Tokens and values are activated into actors: Nature *does* rather than *is*.

♦ Location circumstances are treated as actors, so the environment is less marginalised.

♦ In brief, Nature is seen as a communicator and as active, not inert.

(3) For Goatly, ergative verbs (such as *ring*, *spin*, *sweep*) are used to reflect a natural landscape possessing its own energy irrespective of human beings. How do ergative verbs manage this? To appreciate how they are able to do this, consider the following:

	Ian	drinks.	
	subject	[intransitive]	

Ian	drinks	the water.
subject	[transitive]	object

Drink is a verb that can be used transitively or intransitively, as the above shows. Both transitive and intransitive versions have the same subject. However, a clause such as:

* the water drinks

is semantically aberrant. It needs a human or, more generally speaking, an animate subject. (It might be used in some creative activity (e.g. a poem), but this usage would be limited.)

(The use of the asterisk is a convention in linguistics to indicate that particular stretches of language are not possible in a language.)

Now consider the following:

Ian   rang.
subject   [intransitive]

Ian   rang   the bell.
subject   [transitive]   object

The bell   rang.
subject [intransitive]

Ring is a different kind of verb all together. While, like *drink*, it can be used intransitively with a human subject and transitively with a human subject, the object *the bell* in the transitive structure can be used as the subject of *ring* also. Verbs that allow this are known as ergative verbs. When used intransitively, they do not require human participants. Because of this we can focus especially on Nature by making it a subject theme. So with *An Arctic ice-shelf split off* – which has the ergative verb *split off* – we have a focus on Nature without humans, and thus one where Nature can be seen as self-generating. This is why Goatly favours ergative verbs over non-ergative verbs for representing Nature.

ACTIVITY 15 (allow about five minutes)

Since we are faced in the twenty-first century with potentially serious ecological implications for the planet, a desire to emphasise Nature via intransitive ergatives may be laudable. But can you see any problems with using ergatives for this purpose, particularly in the times we live in as opposed to Wordsworth's time? Think of the example I just gave – *An Arctic ice-shelf split off*.

COMMENT

While *An Arctic ice-shelf split off* has the ergative verb *split off*, in using an ergative to represent this as a self-generated process we do not see who the actor is. At the moment in the Arctic, huge amounts of ice are melting and falling into the surrounding ocean, raising sea-levels. Disastrous results could ensue in the next few decades for certain countries which are mostly at sea-level. The actors of the ice melting are human beings – through our use of industry, our use of cars, etc., which warm the atmosphere with carbon pollution. Indeed, a more representative version ironically would be the transitive one – *Human global warming splits off an Arctic ice-shelf* – although one unlikely to show up in a corpus. *An Arctic ice-shelf splits off* may be ergative and emphasise Nature, but it rather avoids the guilty party.

ACTIVITIES **CD-ROM**   (allow about two hours)

Now work through the activities for this unit on the Activities CD-ROM.

Conclusion

In trying to ascertain the angle on the world in a text, we make an interpretation of a text. To produce a robust interpretation – which has some likelihood that emphasis in a text will affect how experiential meanings are realised by readers generally – we need to anchor interpretation as much as possible in a detailed description of a text. Otherwise, we might be accused of just making impressionistic remarks about the text. We need to be able to point systematically to textual evidence. Analogy with archaeology is helpful. Excavation involves a careful unearthing of evidence from different areas of an archaeological site. It is difficult to stop our human propensity to form hunches. So archaeologists will form hunches about the artefacts they dig up, estimating the period they come from, etc. But these hunches will not be given proper credence until the site has been described comprehensively. Only then will archaeologists begin to extend their hunches into an informed, holistic and systematic interpretation of the artefacts found and their place within the culture.

By analogy, this unit has shown you how to practise and extend your skills of textual description and thus to better ground your interpretations of texts. As with an archaeological site, once a text has been comprehensively described, selective and impressionistic responses are more likely to be avoided.

Learning outcomes

After completing Unit 11, you should have developed your knowledge and understanding of:

◆ the concept of field
◆ how texts can be configured to present a particular angle on experience
◆ the concepts of participant and process, understanding that there are different types.

You should have developed your ability to:

◆ *describe* grammatical features of a text in relation to the concept of field
◆ *interpret* texts and their grammatical features with regard to field.

Finally, let us sum up the aspects of field covered so far:

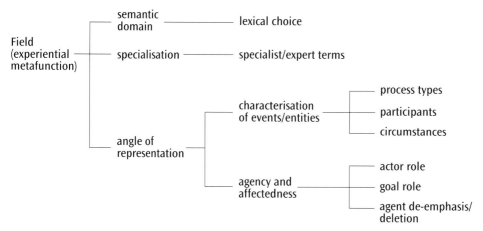

Figure 2 Map of field

Key terms introduced and revisited	
actor	object
angle of representation	participant
circumstance	passivisation
clausal circumstance	process
end-weight	receiver
ergative verb	recipient [beneficiary]
experience [phenomenon]	sayer
experiencer [senser]	short passive
experiential metafunction	subject
given information	subordination
goal [affected]	textual metafunction
information flow	thematisation
interpersonal metafunction	theme
intransitive	token
lexeme [lemma]	transitive
long passive	transitivity analysis
marked theme	value
new information	verbiage
nominalisation	

Near equivalents are given in [ ].

Answers to the activities

ACTIVITY 3

(*Pa* = Participant, *C* = Circumstance, *Pr* = Process)

1   Suddenly, (*C – in what way*), reporters (*Pa*) heard (*Pr*) the crack of shotguns (*Pa*) in the streets (*C – location*). [Transitive]

Note that *the crack of shotguns* stays together as a single chunk. What was it that the reporters heard? – *the crack of shotguns*, not just *the crack* or *shotguns*. Thus *the crack of shotguns* is a participant.

2   The police (*Pa*) fired (*Pr*) wildly (*C – in what way*) at demonstrators (*C – location*). [Intransitive]

Notice here that the chunk which follows the process, *fired*, begins with the preposition *at* – *at demonstrators*. This is one of the indicators that this chunk is a circumstance rather than a participant. As a general rule, participants do not occur as prepositional phrases (chunks beginning with prepositions). Rather, as we saw in Book 1, they occur with noun phrases.
The meaning of *at demonstrators* also gives us a clue. It is performing a typical circumstantial role, indicating where.

3   The protesters (*Pa*) were demonstrating (*Pr*) against Britain's role in the recent airstrikes (*C – in respect of what/for what purpose*). [Intransitive]

The clause divides into the three chunks: *The protesters* (1) + *were demonstrating* (2) + *against Britain's role in the recent air strikes* (3). Various tests indicate that all the words in *against Britain's role in the recent airstrikes* must stay together and hence constitute a single grammatical unit. Thus

> It was against Britain's role in the recent air strikes that the protesters were demonstrating

is fine, while any further divisions of *against Britain's role in the recent air strikes* are not possible. For example:

> * It was in the recent airstrikes that the protesters were demonstrating against Britain's role.

> * It was against Britain's role that the protesters were demonstrating in the recent airstrikes.

(The use of the asterisk is a convention in linguistics to indicate that particular stretches of language are not possible in a language.)

The clause in number 3 is intransitive for reasons similar to those which applied in Activity 2. The chunk (*against Britain's role in the recent airstrikes*) which follows the process begins with the preposition *against* and hence must be a circumstance rather than a participant. As well, if we remove this chunk to produce, *The protesters were demonstrating*, the new clause is grammatical and the words left behind retain their original meanings.

4   Rounds of birdshot (*Pa*) injured (*Pr*) three people (*Pa*) severely (*C – in what way*). [Transitive]

5   Police (*Pa*) used (*Pr*) strong-arm tactics (*Pa*) against the protesters (*C – to what end*). [Transitive]

6   The British prime minister (*Pa*) was attending (*Pr*) an awards ceremony (*Pa*). [Transitive]

7   Police (*Pa*) also used (*Pr*) rubber bullets, stun-grenades and teargas (*Pa*). [Transitive]

Notice that the second participant here contains multiple sub-elements – rubber bullets + stun-grenades + teargas. Reorganisation tests would once again reveal that these words must stay together.

8   They (*Pa*) were vigorously (*C – in what way*) brandishing (*Pr*) threatening placards (*Pa*). [Transitive]

Notice here that the chunk which describes the process (*were brandishing*) has been broken up by means of the intervening circumstance, *vigorously*. It is a special property of such 'adverbs' of manner that they can act in this way and interrupt chunks which would otherwise stay together.

9   Police (*Pa*) used (*Pr*) apartheid-era security laws (*Pa*) against the demonstrators (*C – where, to what end*). [Transitive]

10 A smaller demonstration at the airport (*Pa*) passed off (*Pr*) peacefully (*C – in what way*). [Intransitive]

Passed off is a phrasal verb – the two words cannot be subdivided because the meaning of *pass off* is not a combination of *pass* and *off*:

   * It was off that a smaller demonstration at the airport passed peacefully.

and

   * It was off peacefully that a smaller demonstration at the airport passed.

The meaning of *passed off* is similar to *went* as in *The demonstration went peacefully*. Notice that there is no second participant, just the adverb *peacefully* indicating the manner in which the demonstration *passed off* – a typical circumstantial function.

(For a more detailed take on transitive patterns, but from a more structural rather than functional perspective, see your reference grammar, section 5.7.)

ACTIVITY 8

The intransitive clauses are as follows:

(5) {demonstrators} (*actor*) baying (*process*) for the Prime Minister's blood (*circumstances/purpose/cause*).

(Here, of course, the demonstrators are being compared, via metaphor, to an action that dogs do. The process of *baying* is an intransitive one – it has an actor, the demonstrators, but no entity is directly acted upon.)

(10) moments before shooting (*actor*) broke out (*process – phrasal verb*).

(19) {in order for the crowd} (*actor*) to disperse (*process*).

(22) They {the police} (*actor*) then opened fire (*process – phrasal verb*).

(24) Officers (*actor*) took deliberate aim (*process – phrasal verb*) with shotguns (*circumstance/means*).

(It might be possible to treat this as transitive with *Officers* as actor, *took* as process and *deliberate aim* as goal. However, I believe that *take aim* can be treated as a phrasal verb as a chunk which operates together to indicate the action. Accordingly I treat this as intransitive.)

(25) as others [[armed with automatic rifles]] (*actor*) crouched (*process*) with their weapons at the ready (*circumstance/manner*).

(33) {a reporter} (*actor*) running (*process*) for cover (*circumstance/location or purpose*).

(36) and {ordinary civilians} (*actor*) dived (*process*) for cover (*circumstance/location or purpose*) behind an ornamental wall (*circumstance/location*).

(It might alternatively be possible to treat *dive for cover* as a phrasal verb.)

(40) and {Mr Blair} (*actor*) continued (*process*) with his programme (*circumstance*).

(45) police and ambulance sirens (*actor*) wailing (*process*) through the city (*circumstance/location*).

ACTIVITY 9

1   Transitive and long passive material process clauses:

(1) Transitive: <u>Bullets</u> (*actor*) <u>wreck</u> (*process*) <u>Blair visit</u> (*goal*).

(4) Transitive: <u>men</u> (*actor*) <u>handing out</u> (*process – phrasal verb*) <u>guns</u> (*goal*) <u>to demonstrators</u> (*recipient*).

> This process involves three participants rather than just two: an actor, a goal and a recipient or beneficiary. Such three-process structures most typically occur with verbs of transfer. The verb *to give* is perhaps the prototypical ditransitive – thus: *He* (actor) *gave* (process) *me* (recipient) *the menu* (goal); *He* (actor) *gave* (process) *the menu* (goal) *to the customer* (recipient).

(6) Long passive: <u>Mr Blair's convoy of cars</u> (*goal*) <u>had been held up</u> (*process – phrasal verb*) <u>by the demonstration</u> (*by-phrase actor*).

(7) Long passive: {<u>demonstration</u>} (*goal*) <u>organised</u> (*process*) <u>by a group</u> (*by-phrase actor*).

(13) Transitive/ditransitive: <u>two men</u> (*actor*) <u>distributing</u> (*process*) <u>arms</u> (*goal*) <u>to protesters</u> (*recipient*).

(14) Transitive: <u>who</u> {<u>protesters</u>} (*actors*) <u>held up</u> (*process – phrasal verb*) <u>placards</u> (*goal*).

(18) Transitive/ditransitive: that <u>they</u> (*actor*) <u>gave</u> (*process*) <u>the crowd</u> (*recipient*) <u>five minutes</u> (*goal*).

> Notice that this is another ditransitive of transfer. Notice as well that this process does not actually involve a physical action – there was actually no physical transfer of *five minutes* to *the crowd*. The actual meaning here is something like *The police told the protesters that they should disperse in five minutes.*

(20) Transitive: <u>before</u> {<u>the police</u>} (*actor*) <u>firing</u> (*process*) <u>teargas</u> (*goal*).

(21) Transitive: and {<u>the police</u>} (*actor*) <u>throwing</u> (*process*) <u>stun grenades</u> (*goal*) <u>at the demonstrators</u> (*circumstance/location*).

(27) Transitive: <u>the police</u> (*actor*) <u>did not use</u> (*process*) <u>sharp-point ammunition</u> (*goal*).

> Notice that there is actually no agency here due to the negation *did not...*

(30) Long passive: and <u>a woman</u> (*goal*) <u>grazed</u> (*process*) <u>on the head</u> (*circumstance/location*) <u>by a bullet</u> (*by-phrase actor*).

(34) Long passive: and <u>a reporter</u> (*goal*) <u>was shot</u> (*process*) <u>in the legs</u> (*circumstance/location*) <u>by a police gun</u> (*by-phrase actor*).

(35) Transitive: Ordinary civilians (*actor*) fled (*process*) the scene (*range – see note below*).

> Strictly speaking *the scene* is not a goal. Under the functional system of grammar it would be an instance of a process type that has not been discussed. Notice that *the scene* here is clearly not an entity that is being acted upon, affected or even targeted by the process of *fleeing*. Rather it indicates the location from which the fleeing took place. As a consequence the *ordinary civilians* are not represented here as acting upon or affecting any second party or entity – they clearly do not affect *the scene* in any way. Such location-indicating objects are termed ranges under the functional system.

(37) Transitive: as the demonstrators (*actor*)... attempted to hide (*process*) their firearms (*goal*).

(38) Transitive: some of them women (*actor*) wearing (*process*) long dresses (*goal*).

(41) Transitive: {Mr Blair} (*actor*) presenting (*process*) British soldiers (*recipient*) with medals (*goal*) for their work... (*circumstance/cause*).

> Notice that *present* is a transfer verb which typically occurs with a goal (the thing transferred) and a recipient (the entity towards which the transfer is directed). Notice that here the goal has been atypically realised via the prepositional phrase 'with medals' rather than with a noun phrase.

(42) Transitive: {British soldiers} (*actor*) retraining (*process*) the South African Army (*goal*).

2 Short/agentless passive material process clauses:

(2) FOUR people (*goal*) were wounded (*process*) in a gunfight between political extremists and police (*circumstance/location*) about 100 yards from Tony Blair (*circumstance/location*) in Cape Town (*circumstance/location*) yesterday (*circumstance/time*).

(9) and he (*goal*) was smuggled (*process*) in through a side entrance of the Castle (*circumstance/location*).

(23) after {the police} (*goal*) being shot at (*process*) themselves (*repeats and hence emphasises the goal*).

(28) Two members of People Against Gangsterism and Drugs – a vigilante group with its own armed wing – (*goal*) were arrested: (*process*).

(29) a man who (*goal*) had been wounded (*process*) in the neck and shoulder (*circumstance/location*).

(32) and a reporter (*goal*) was caught (*process*) in the crossfire (*circumstance/location*).

ACTIVITY 13

A1

1 American consumers get two-thirds of their fruit from the orchards of California.

Californian orchards supply American consumers with two-thirds of their fruit.

2 Several million people live on the prairies of North America.

The prairies of North America support several million people.

3 Traditional herbalists and their patients obtain useful remedies from the tree bark.

The tree bark benefits traditional herbalists and their patients with its useful remedies.

4 Children pick berries off the bushes.

The bushes succour the children with berries.

5 The wheat crop finds nourishment in the nitrates of the legumes planted the previous year.

The nitrates of the legumes planted the previous year nourish the wheat crop.

A2

6 Organically fertilised rice fields enabled a twofold increase in production.

A twofold increase in production was possible in organically fertilised rice fields.

7 The areas where snakes had been introduced caused a reduction in the rat population.

A reduction in the rat population came about in the areas where snakes had been introduced.

8 The monsoon rain relieved the drought-stricken crops.

The drought-stricken crops began to recover in the monsoon rain.

9 These islands can assist the overspill of human population from the mainland to survive.

The overspill from the mainland can survive on these islands.

10 The coast of Oman can help the fishermen to continue to live.

The fishermen live off the coast of Oman.

B1

1 I concentrated on the eagles for three hours.

The eagles held my concentration for three hours.

2 I noticed the glow worms.

The glow worms caught my attention.

3 I worried about the coming hurricane.

The coming hurricane disturbed me.

4 I looked intently at the birds.

The birds held my gaze.

5 I perceived the sudden movement in the undergrowth.

The sudden movement in the undergrowth attracted my notice.

B2

6 The waterfall riveted his gaze.

He observed the waterfall intently.

7 The trek through the rainforest pleased me.

I liked the trek through the rainforest.

8 The seashore delighted the children.

The children really enjoyed the seashore.

9 The snakes disgusted her.

She hated the snakes.

10 The name of the species of monkey escaped her.

She forgot the name of the species of monkey.

C1

1 Jordan is to the West of Iraq.

Jordan lies to the West of Iraq.

2 The mountain is above the village.

The mountain rears up above the village.

3 The lake is at the foot of the mountain.

The lake sits at the foot of the mountain.

4 The path is beyond the wood.

The path runs beyond the wood.

5   The river was long.

The river stretched a long way.

C2

6   The chasm gaped.

The chasm was very wide.

7   The crevasse yawned ahead of them.

The crevasse was very wide and deep ahead of them.

8   The city sprawls.

The city is large and untidy in its development.

9   The mountain dominates the valley.

The mountain is high above the valley.

Review of Book 2

In this book, building on the mainly structural descriptive approach of Book 1, you have been introduced to the functional analysis of texts. Specifically, Halliday's systemic functional linguistics model has been used as a framework: within this, linguistic communications are seen as simultaneously creating three main types of meaning, or serving three metafunctions: textual (conveying a coherent message), interpersonal (social interaction or exchange) and experiential (representation or construal of events and experiences). These functions of communication are realised by a range of lexicogrammatical forms, which reflect and help to construct three aspects of the context of the communicative event: mode, tenor and field. You have been acquiring practical skills to enable you to carry out a register analysis of a text, for instance determining its mode from the packaging and staging of information in noun phrases and clause themes, its tenor by evaluating the use of modality and personalisation, and its field by looking at choices of active or passive constructions and process types. These three areas will be revisited in greater depth in the next book, which will provide you with additional analytical skills to assess how particular texts make meaning.

In terms of research findings covered, this book has narrowed the focus of Book 1's investigation of broad differences between speech and writing, to examine the four Longman registers of conversation, fiction, news and academic prose. You have seen how these differ lexicogrammatically, for example in the choice of describers and classifiers in noun phrases, in the frequency of thematisation of pronouns or nominalisations or the standing of participants, and in the use of short passives to remove the actor from a representation of events. As well as noting your reference grammar's findings, you have been able to explore some of these differences within the BNC-OU corpus, and will have developed further skills in using the concordancing software to investigate corpus variation and lexico-grammatical patterns. In particular, you have seen how a functional concept like stance can be investigated by using the concordancer to detect a 'global groove' of bias in an individual text or whole corpus. This illustrates how approaches from corpus and functional linguistics can help us better understand how our perception of events may be influenced by the language used to report them – just one way in which grammatical study can have practical value.

Applications (extension study)

If you have time in your study schedule, you may now find it interesting to look at another professional application of some of the concepts and skills you have been developing. Work through Chapter 2 of *Applications: Putting grammar into professional practice* on corpus-based and functional grammar perspectives in English language teaching, 'Putting grammar into educational practice', by Chris Candlin.

This study is **optional** and will not be compulsorily assessed.

Key terms from Book 2

As for Book 1, to help remember and revise terms introduced or revisited in this book, you may find it useful to try to write brief definitions of a few words selected from this list. Contrast each term with other related terms where relevant, e.g. **tenor** vs. **field** and **mode**, and think of a couple of examples to illustrate the concept, e.g. *I ate the cake*; *The cake was eaten (by me)* as instances of goals in material process clauses. If you are unsure about any of your definitions or examples, use the index to Book 2 and/or Book 1 to look up fuller discussions of the concepts. The separate course *Glossary* may also provide useful short definitions and examples of some terms, and your reference grammar will be helpful for certain concepts from *structural* grammar (though many new terms introduced in this book are from *functional* grammar and so will not feature in the reference grammar, or will have slightly different meanings there).

actor	angle of representation	attitude	circumstance
classifier	clausal circumstance	collocation	complement clause
congruent	context of use	deictic	deontic modality
determiner	dialogic	end-weight (principle)	epistemic modality
ergative verb	experience [phenomenon]	experiencer [senser]	experiential metafunction
experiential theme [topical theme]	field	given information	goal [affected]
grammatical metaphor	head	information flow (principle)	interactivity
interpersonal metafunction	interpersonal theme	interpersonalisation	intensifier
interrogative	intransitive	it-clause	lexeme [lemma]

long passive	Longman register	marked theme	modal adjective
modal adverb	modal finite [modal verb]	mode	mood
new information	nominalisation	numerative	object
paradigmatic meaning	participant	passivisation	persona
personalisation	polar interrogative	positioning	process
productive	qualifier	rank scale	receiver
recipient [beneficiary]	register	register analysis	relative social status
relator	rheme	sayer	semantic domain
short passive	social distance	speaker / writer persona	spontaneity
stance [modality in SFL]	standing	subject	subordination
syntagmatic (meaning)	synthetic personalisation	systemic functional linguistics [SFL]	taxonomy
tenor	textual metafunction	textual theme	thematisation
theme	thing	token	transitive
transitivity analysis	unmarked theme	value	verbiage
wh-interrogative	word frequency		

Near equivalents are given in [ ].

References

'Australian Identity', *Write it Right* (1996) Erskineville (Aus.), Disadvantaged Schools Program, NSW Department of School Education.

Bell, A. (1991) *The Language of News Media*, Oxford, Blackwell.

Biber, D. and Conrad, S. (2004) 'Corpus-based comparisons of registers' in Coffin, C., Hewings, A. and O'Halloran, K. A. (eds) *Applying English Grammar: Functional and Corpus Approaches*, London, Arnold.

Biber, D., Johansson, S., Leech, G., Conrad, S. and Finegan, E. (1999) *The Longman Grammar of Spoken and Written English*, London, Longman.

Collins Cobuild Bank of English: subcorpus = brspok/UK.

'Exploring literacy in school science', *Write it Right* (1996) Erskineville (Aus.), Disadvantaged Schools Program, NSW Department of School Education.

Gittins, M. (1998) 'Computers are bad for you', *PC Basics*, Issue 3, December 1998.

Goatly, A. (2000) *Critical Reading and Writing*, London, Routledge.

Halliday, M. A. K. (1993) 'Some grammatical problems in scientific English' in *Writing Science: Literacy and Discursive Power*, Halliday, M. A. K. and Martin, J. R. (eds), London, Falmer.

Heffernan, D. A. and Learmouth, M. S. (1988) *The World of Science: Book One*, Melbourne, Longman Cheshire

Hemingway, E. (1980) *The Essential Hemingway*, London, Granada.

Hewings, A. and Hewings, M. (2004) 'Impersonalising stance: a study of anticipatory "it" in student and published academic writing' in Coffin, C., Hewings, A. and O'Halloran, K. A. (eds) *Applying English Grammar: Functional and Corpus Approaches*, London, Arnold.

Kavanagh, T. and Lea, M. (2003) 'The same two you, Prescott', *The Sun*, 6 June 2003.

Kiley, S. and Sherman, J. (1999) 'Bullets wreck Blair visit', *The Times*, 9 January 1999.

Murdoch, I. (1978) *The Sea, The Sea*, London, Chatto & Windus.

Osborne, C. K., Zhao, H. and Fuqua, S. A. (2000) 'Selective estrogen receptor modulators: structure, function, and clinical use', *Journal of Clinical Oncology*, 18 (17): September 2000; 3172–86. Quoted in PubMed website [accessed 11 August 2003].

Pascoe-Watson, G. (2003) 'Two million jobs in peril', *The Sun*, 27 May 2003.

Russell, A. (2003) 'Cure SARS', *The Sun*, 16 April 2003.

South China Morning Post [editorial] (2003) 'For Hong Kong, a time of soul-searching', *South China Morning Post*, 15 April 2003. Available from http://www.scmp.com [accessed 20 September 2003].

Acknowledgements

Unit 8

Text

Russell, A. (2003) 'Turnips cure SARS', *The Sun*, 16 April 2003. News International Newspapers, Limited. Copyright © 2003 News Group Newspapers Ltd.

South China Morning Post (2003) 'For Hong Kong, a time for soul-searching', 15 April 2003. South China Morning Post Publishers Ltd. Hong Kong.

Unit 9

Text

Extract Russell, A. (2003) 'Turnips cure SARS', *The Sun*, 16 April 2003. News International Newspapers, Limited. Copyright © 2003 News Group Newspapers Ltd.

Unit 10

Text

Pascoe-Watson, G. (2003) '2 million jobs in peril', *The Sun*, 27 May 2003. News International Newspapers, Limited. Copyright © 2003 News Group Newspapers Ltd.

Unit 11

Text

Kiley, S. and Sherman, J. (1999) 'Bullets wreck Blair visit', *The Times*, 9 January, 1999. News International Newspapers, Limited. Copyright © 1999 News Group Newspapers Ltd.

Course team acknowledgements

The course team wish to thank and acknowledge the assistance of the following in the publication of this book.

Michael Hoey (external assessor)

Ron Carter, Susan Feez, Michael Halliday, Geoffrey Leech (general course consultants)

Elena Tognini-Bonelli (adviser)

Tarek Fakhrel-Deen, Mohammad Awwad, Lewis Mukattash (Arab OU critical readers)

Judy Anderson, Frank Xiao Junhong, Ahmed Sahlane, Susana Cerda (developmental testers)

E303 Associate Lecturers, particularly Marisa Lohr (revisions to course materials)

Index

Page references in bold type refer to the most significant treatment of the subject, italics refer to meanings and 'f' indicates a figure